A Living History of

America, Land of Opportunity

AMERICAN HISTORY AND GOVERNMENT FOR THE HIGH SCHOOL STUDENT

Written and Illustrated by Angela O'Dell

No part of this book may be copied or stored without express, written permission from the author.

© Jellybeanjar Publications™
2015

Many thanks to the homeschooled students,
who allowed me to use their pictures
on the covers of this course

Zoe Anderson, on the front cover of this book,
Joseph Merboth, on the front cover of
the Student Journal,
and
Abby Sorensen, on the back cover of the
Student Journal

American History and Government for the High School Student
America, Land of Opportunity

"A primary object should be the education of our youth in the science of government. In a republic, what species of knowledge can be equally important? And what duty more pressing than communicating it to those who are to be the future guardians of the liberties of the country?"

A Living History of Our World

This book is dedicated to the great Americans,
past and present,
who inspire me to dig deep

A special thank you to
Steve Lambert & Dr. Gary Newton,
Bless you both!

Soli Deo Gloria

Angela O'Dell

It is a joy and a privilege to provide this high school level study of our
country's history and government.
It has been quite a journey
and one that has reminded me
of how many great people dot the landscape of our past.
My heart is full. There are no words to express my gratitude for their bravery.
As you join me in this study, I pray that you will see God's hand on our
country's path - past and present.
Enjoy the journey!

An extra special thank you to
Kyrsten Carlson & Renee O'Dell, for your much-appreciated
help with proof reading and editing.

Resource Lists and Note to Parent

Required Resource List

- Encyclopedias (book or cd rom) or internet availability for research
- An atlas with maps worthy of tracing or printable maps from the internet
- Highlighters
- A spiral notebook for extra notes, writing assignments, and vocabulary words
- Regular sized file folders and several large poster boards (at least 4)

These resources will be required throughout the year as you construct your "Map Work and Geography Notebook."

1. A 1-inch, three-ring, binder-style notebook (We especially like the kind with the clear plastic sleeve on the cover. A decorative title page is included in this Student Journal.)

2. If you wish to preserve your map projects without hole punching them, you will need a package of at least 20 page protectors.

3. If you wish to print out maps on which to complete the map projects, you will need: a printer and printer paper.

4. If you wish to trace your own maps from an atlas, you will need: a pad of high-quality tracing paper, a package of white card stock, clear tape, paper clips, an extremely thin-line, black, permanent pen (at least one).

5. Whether you print or trace your maps, you will also need colored pencils to color them, and if you wish, fine-tipped markers for outlining.

Optional Resource List (* Indicates HIGHLY recommended)

- *1828 Webster's Dictionary - available through many, larger homeschool supply providers
- Drive Thru History Foundations of Character - available through many, larger homeschool supply providers
- *Mr. Smith Goes to Washington (DVD - James Stewart, 1939)
- Wall Builders American Heritage DVD series
- For You They Signed by Marilyn Boyer
- A complete copy of the Federalist Papers - available at most large bookstores (or free online)

Resource Lists and Note to Parent

Dear Parent,

As your student completes this course, please keep track of their progress. If you are keeping grades for your student's transcripts, here is an idea for a grading system:

25% of total grade based upon student's attitude and responsibility taken for the course work.

50% of total grade based upon student's thoroughness in written summaries and deeper research.

25% of total grade based upon mid-term and end of year exam.

Introduction

"And may God grant that His grace may really affect your heart with suitable impressions of His goodness. Remember that God made you, that God keeps you alive and preserves you from all harm, and gives you all the powers and the capacity whereby you are able to read of Him and of Jesus Christ, your Savior and Redeemer, and to do every other needful business of life. And while you look around you and see the great privileges and advantages you have above what other children have (of learning to read and write, of being taught the meaning of the great truths of the Bible), you must remember not to be proud on that account but to bless God and be thankful and endeavor in your turn to assist others with the knowledge you may gain." Written by Henry Marchant (to his daughter), member of the Continental Congress, Attorney General of Rhode Island, ratifier of the U.S. Constitution, Federal Judge appointed by President George Washington.*

Dear student of history,

I have personally read and studied our founding days from what we now call ultra-conservative, conservative, moderate, liberal, and left-wing liberal viewpoints. During these times of research, I was struck with how various groups of individuals, holding to a certain viewpoint, are stubbornly resistant to the consideration of any other opinions, even though original documentation begs to differ with their tightly-held viewpoint. The discovery of this stubborn resistance is puzzling to me. Why wouldn't you want to know the truth about something? Especially about something so easily researched? There are letters and journal entries, penned by the hands of many Founding Fathers, which are available for us to study today.

Because I write every book with the goal of encouraging deeper thinking, and therefore, I am stating it loudly and clearly right here at the beginning of this book: I do not want to tell you, as the student, what or how to think. I will share with you what I have come to see, through my research, but I will not (as I CANNOT!) think for you. With this in mind, please read through the following list of presuppositions, but remember that I encourage you to *prove* them to be true. Also keep in mind, although you are responsible for forming your own opinions, these opinions must be based on unbiased fact as much as possible - fact gathered from firsthand accounts. It is to this end that you will be studying

Introduction

many original documents and speeches, and as you do so, you will be researching and defining the original words and phrases. As you work through these great historical documents, you will be seeing with your own eyes the principles on which our country was founded.

This book is written based upon these presuppositions:
- Although not everyone in American history was a Christian, our roots are much more ethical and moral than our current cultural climate.
- My research has shown me that although the Founding Fathers came from mixed religious backgrounds and views, the Bible was commonly used as a moral compass in the making of laws and the establishing of various governmental offices and duties.
- My research also shows that many of the signers of the Constitution were godly men, with a wholesome fear of the LORD Almighty. In fact, more than half of the signers held seminary degrees (among other degrees and titles).
- The hotly debated topic of separation of church and state originated to protect the people from an oppressive, government ordered religion. Its purpose was to keep the government out of the business of the nation's churches. It was never purposed to remove God from the government, the culture, or from people's lives.

You will be using the following list of skills in the completion of this course.
- Researching
- Note-taking
- Writing narrations (summaries)
- Answering essay questions
- Mapping projects
- Thinking critically
- Conducting word and document study

Many blessings,

Angela O'Dell

"Duty is ours; results are God's." John Quincy Adams

*Letters of Delegates to Congress: May 1, 1777 - September 18, 1777, Paul H. Smith, editor (Washington DC: Library of Congress, 1981), Vol. 7, pp. 645-646, Henry Marchant to Sarah Marchant on September 9, 1777.

Table of Contents

Chapter	page
1: Early European Explorers	13
2: The Colonial Period Part 1	19
3: The Colonial Period Part 2	24
4: The French and Indian War	29
5: Rebellion Against Tyranny and Oppression	37
6: The Revolutionary War: Part 1	45
7: The Revolutionary War: Part 2	54
8: The Treaty of Paris and the Confederation of the Colonies	62
9: The Constitutional Convention	69
10: The Founders and Framers Part 1	75
11: The Founders and Framers Part 2	80
12: The Great Debate: Federalists versus Anti-Federalist	84
13: The Branches of Government, the Legislative Branch	89
14: The Branches of Government, the Legislative Branch	93
15: The Branches of Government, the Executive Branch	97
16: The Branches of Government, the Judicial Branch	100
17: More About Our Government and Constitution	105
18: Our Changing Country	113
19: The War of 1812 & the Jacksonian Period	118
20: America Grows and Changes	123
21: A Country Divided	129
22: The War Between the States Part 1	133
23: The War Between the States Part 2	139
24: Reconstruction	145
25: The Big Business Boom	149
26: The Turn of the Century	153
27: The Election Process Part 1	161

Table of Contents

28: The Election Process Part 2 — 166
29: America and the Great War — 171
30: The Roaring Twenties & the Dirty Thirties — 182
31: America in World War 2 — 188
32: America in the Last 50 Years — 168

Conscientious Conclusion Project — 195
Work Cited — 197
Teacher's Notes — 199

Colonial America
1492 - 1763

Chapter 1: Early European Explorers

Chapter 2: The Colonial Period - Part 1

Chapter 3: The Colonial Period - Part 2

Chapter 4: The French and Indian War

Please leave blank.

Chapter 1 — Early European Explorers

America has not always been the Land of Opportunity; several centuries ago, it was nothing but wild land, mostly untouched by human hands. The only inhabitants of this immense continent were tribes of people, living as part of the earth itself. These people groups did not view the land as something that they could own - this thought was as foreign to them as trying to own the air they breathed. They did not try to change the earth, but instead, they lived governed by the seasons, many of them moving from one place to another when winter or drought brought an end to their regular food supplies.

Although it is certainly not the true beginning of America's history, we are going to begin our study of American history at the point in time where the European explorers first found their way to our shores. This is, in no way, meant as a slight to the millions of inhabitants who populated the great American continents before the Europeans' arrival. In fact, there is so much pre-European history to uncover, I could easily fill several volumes outlining that time period alone. However, because the focus of this volume is more centered around the making of the United States of America and our government, and because time and page numbers are limited, I am choosing to focus on the post-European discovery era.

* * * * * * * * * * * * * *

On the fateful day in 1492, when Columbus and his crew, financially backed by the famous King Ferdinand and Queen Isabella of Spain, landed on the small island in the Bahamas archipelago, the door of exploration was flung open to what would soon be called "The New World." Although Columbus was at first convinced that he had reached the islands of Japan or someplace nearby, it soon became apparent that he had, indeed, stumbled across an unexplored continent. Columbus was only the first of many European explorers. As the rumors of vast riches in the New World spread like wildfire across Europe, the race was on; each country sent its best and bravest men to explore and claim large tracts of land for their respective mother countries. Rulers of Europe knew that whoever could claim and

Chapter 1

settle the biggest section of the New World could quite possibly become the most powerful nation on earth.

"Columbus discovered a continent; an impostor gave it his name. In 1503 an Italian adventurer, Amerigo Vespucci, published an account of a 'new world' which he claimed have discovered in 1497. The whole story was a fabrication. But a young German professor, who was publishing a geography at the time, named the new continent America, *after the dishonest author of the fictitious discovery."* (1)

When Ferdinand and Isabella of Spain had originally agreed to finance Columbus' expedition, their ultimate goal was to find a more direct and timely route to the Orient. China, Japan, and even India were known to be immensely wealthy, a fact that enticed the Spanish king and queen to want to open better trading routes and therefore fill their royal treasury.

Columbus had not been able to find any great treasure on his expeditions, causing Ferdinand and Isabella to see the immense landmass as a roadblock; their main attention was still focused upon establishing a satisfactory trading relationship and route between themselves and the Orient. This desire to find a route through the Americas kept many of the Spanish explorers traveling up and down the length of the newly discovered continents in search for a passage way. Even though the Americas were now on the map, there was no way to know just how immense they were. I am sure if Ferdinand and Isabella knew the size of the landmasses that they were trying to pass through and the massive expanse of the Pacific Ocean on the other side, they would have given up looking for a trade route through them.

While it was an Spanish explorer, Vasco de Balboa, who explored and crossed the Isthmus of Panama in 1513, and another, Ferdinand Magellan, who circumnavigated the earth between the years 1519 and 1522, other Spanish explorers traversed into the Americas, fueled by the hopes of finding the much sought after gold of the

> **F.Y.I**
> The country of Spain was struggling financially, mostly due to their many, long years of war against the Muslim raiders.

14

Chapter 1

New World. These fortune seeking explorers were called conquistadores (or conquerers). Their early expeditions in the New World remained mostly along the coast of South and Central America. When they tired of their searchings along the coast, the conquistadores turned their attention inland.

The two most famous of these conquistadores were Francisco Pizarro and Hernando Cortés, and they both played an enormously important part in establishing the rule of Spain over a vast portion of the New World. Francisco Pizarro was enticed by the reports of the riches in the New World. His focus, however, was on the great Incan empire of Peru. In 1532, Pizarro overthrew the Incan leader, Atahualpa, and conquered Peru. Three years later, in 1535, he founded the city of Lima, the new capital.

Hernando Cortés landed in what is now Mexico (but at that time was the great Aztec empire) in the same year that Magellan began his famous voyage around the earth. Cortés, a rather gutsy fellow, marched on Tenochititlan, the capital city of the Aztec empire. The Aztec king, Montezuma, thinking these Spaniards were gods, welcomed them into his city. Cortés captured Montezuma, defeated the Aztec warriors, and destroyed the city of Tenochititlan. The ruins became the building site for a new city called Mexico City. Historians have argued long and furiously about the Spanish conquistadors' treatment of the native Central Americans. Some berate the barbaric way the Spanish came and destroyed the Aztec civilization, leaving behind nothing but absolute ruin. Others consider these actions to be consistent with the behavior of thousands of other conquering nations before them.

As the Spanish were exploring the New World, the English were also financing their own explorations into America. England's activity in the Americas angered Spain, who believed that they owned these new lands, because it had been their explorers who first found them. England disagreed, of course, and retaliated by plundering Spanish gold ships. English sea captains seemed to be a different breed of human beings, willing to risk their lives in daring and bold attacks on ships twice the size of their own. These dare-devil ship captains earned the name "Sea Dogs" because of their pirating ways. Spain watched in outraged disbelief as they raided coastal towns, seized Spanish ships, and stole the gold coming from Central America.

Chapter 1

During the 1500s, the long-prevailing tension between England and France mounted until it erupted into a famous battle between England's Queen Elizabeth I and Spain's King Phillip II. England's smaller, faster, and more maneuverable warships, commanded by the famous "Sea Dogs," inflicted major damage on Spain's veritable floating fortresses. This battle was important for many reasons, and we will explore several of them.

Queen Elizabeth I of England, was a Protestant. The Reformation had spread throughout Europe, and England had fought its way through the Dark Ages, finding herself in an era of new hope and freedom. The citizens of England rightly acknowledged that it was their "Good Queen Bess," who had worked hard to bring them to this point. Spain, along with its king, Phillip II, was a strongly Roman Catholic nation. Phillip II saw all Protestant nations as a threat to his dream of a Catholic Europe, and his attention was specifically drawn to England for more personal reasons. You see, Phillip II had, at one time, been the king of England.

Before Queen Elizabeth I had come to the throne, her sister, known as "Bloody Mary," had been queen of England. Mary had chosen a husband to rule by her side and, hopefully, produce an heir to the throne. This husband was none other than Phillip II of Spain, who at that time, was a prince. When Mary died at the age of forty-two from an unknown type of cancer, she did not leave an heir, and Phillip II lost his English royal position. When Elizabeth was brought forth to be crowned queen, Phillip II offered to marry her, but the good queen would not consider it for a moment.

Phillip II returned home to his royal position in Spain. It is safe to say that he and Elizabeth never saw eye to eye on anything, from politics to religion. So, now these

Chapter 1

two feuding royals and their respective countries were fighting over lands in the New World. After the English Sea Dogs tromped all over his Spanish warships, Phillip II knew that his nation's navy was no longer considered master of the sea. England's victory had placed them at the top, and more importantly, opened the New World for Protestant settlements. It would be because of these Protestant English's claims in America that the way would be clear for religious pilgrims to come to the New World.

The New World had also caught the eye of the French but for a different reason. Because the Spanish had a strong hold on the Caribbean area and Central America, the French sent explorers to focus more on major sections of North America. Like Spain (and many other European countries), France was interested in finding a route through the continents to the Far East. Jacques Cartier (CAR-tee-AY) was a French explorer, who was searching for such a passageway and in the process, found the St. Lawrence River. This exciting discovery led to France's claim of a large portion of Northern America.

Another French explorer, Robert de La Salle claimed the Mississippi River. At first, he thought he was on a westwardly flowing river that would lead him to the coast of the continent and ultimately, to the Pacific Ocean. Eventually, he realized that he was heading south, instead of west, and by the time he reached the delta region, where the "Mighty Mississip" exits into the Gulf of Mexico, he knew that he had discovered one of the wonderful treasures of this new continent.

Unlike the English and Spanish, the French settlements in the New World were not well organized. Throughout the seventeenth century, the French established trade with the Native American Indians. Their settlements were predominately trading posts and forts deep in the wilderness. The rivers and lakes of the northlands proved to be useful as roads for them to travel from one settlement to another and to transport their furs. Some of these settlements, including Quebec, Montreal, and Detroit in the north, and New Orleans in the south, became key locations for trading with the Indians, and for housing the French soldiers stationed in America to protect France's interests. Because of the nature of the French settlements in America, peaceful settlers were not especially drawn to them. Added to the uninviting prospect of living with a rough trapper population was the fact that the French settlements

Chapter 1

were only open to French Roman Catholics. The only non-Catholic settlers allowed to live in the French settlements were the Huguenots, an industrious and highly skilled group of rogue Protestants, who had been forced to flee France for religious reasons.

Although there were other European countries who sent explorers to the New World, it was the English, Spanish, and French who had the major holdings in the Americas by the end of the sixteenth century. The Spanish concentrated mostly on mining the natural resources of the New World, while the French cornered the market in the fur trading industry, but as we will learn in the next chapter, the English gained a leading position with a completely different approach in developing their claims in America.

Chapter 2   The Colonial Period - Part 1

As the Spanish mined for gold and other precious metals, and the French traversed the waters of the northern lakes and rivers, with their canoes heaped with furs, the English interests lay in establishing permanent settlements. Their dream was to open up the New World to regular citizens, to make it possible to live a normal life in comfortable homes.

Throughout the late 1500s, several settlements were established, but they did not last. Inclement weather, severe famine, poor leadership, and hostile Indians proved to be too much for the first small settlement established on Roanoke Island off of the coast of North Carolina in 1585. Sir Walter Raleigh, an English nobleman who organized the settlement, would not give up, and in 1587, he placed John White in charge of a new colony.

After establishing his group, White returned to England for supplies, not knowing that the war with Spain would keep him from returning to the little colony for three years. When John White finally returned to America, the colony on Roanoke Island was completely gone. The inhabitants had disappeared without a trace, leaving only one clue, the word "Croatan" carved into a tree. John White was frantic. His daughter and baby granddaughter, Virginia Dare, the first English child to be born in America, were among the missing. Had the nearby tribe of Croatan Indians killed everyone, or perhaps, taken them captive? To this day, no one knows for sure what happened to the "Lost Colony" of Roanoke Island.

It wasn't until nearly twenty years later, in 1607, that England was finally able to establish a permanent settlement in America. The settlers of this colony were sent from England, financially backed by wealthy, English merchants, to establish a moneymaking settlement. The group, which consisted of a little over one hundred men and boys, many from the upper class, arrived in the New World with high expectations and little skill. These men were accustomed to servants doing the dirty work of life, and they had no idea how to plant gardens, build houses, or survive in the brutal cold of winter. The location of the colony was rather dubious, also. Situated in a low-lying, marshy region on the James River, the malaria-carrying mosquitoes nearly drove the aristocratic businessmen out of their minds!

Chapter 2

There was one man among them, who knew what had to be done for them in order to survive. John Smith was a rough and rugged man, well accustomed to hard situations. When he attempted to admonish the downtrodden men of the group to pick up their spades and work, they stubbornly refused. It was only when the population had dropped, from the death of the sick and weak, that the remaining men were willing to listen to what John Smith had to say. Smith used II Thessalonians 3:10 as his motto and decreed that whoever among them did not work, would not eat. This command got the men moving, and soon everyone was working to survive.

Through the negotiations of a young Indian girl, named Pocahontas, the nearby Indian tribes also helped supply the Englishmen with enough food to get through that tough winter. Pocahontas was a friend of John Smith, and between the two of them, they were able to maintain peace between the Indians and the Englishmen. It appeared that Jamestown would be a success after all, and hundreds of men from England traveled across the great ocean to join the original band. Eventually there were six hundred men living in the colony.

The following year, John Smith was injured in a gunpowder explosion and had to return to England. After his departure, relations between the settlers and the Indians worsened. Living conditions continued to deteriorate, as a terrible famine plagued the settlement during the winter, causing many deaths. By spring, there were only sixty men left, and they wanted to give up and return to England. Just as they were preparing to set sail, however, ships from England arrived with more colonists and supplies. Jamestown was soon thriving once again, and the dream of making money was revived. All around the colony, a new crop was growing thick and tall, planted with the hopes of making Jamestown wealthy. Tobacco would become almost as valuable to England as the gold of Central America was to Spain. England finally had a permanent and thriving colony in the New World.

With the thriving business and the many hardworking colonists of Jamestown, it made it necessary to form some type of government. The English king, across the ocean, was the true authority, but the colonists realized that they needed to have something in place for the everyday issues that they faced, the kinds of issues the king didn't know anything about, because he didn't live in the New World. The men decided they needed a type of

Chapter 2

representative government, and so the Virginia House of Burgesses began meeting in Jamestown in 1619.

Every late fall, we celebrate the first Thanksgiving in America by stuffing ourselves with turkey and cranberries, pumpkin pie, and green bean casserole. We have all heard the story of the Pilgrims and their colossal struggle to get to the New World and to survive once they got here. You may be familiar with the story of the Pilgrims and the Plymouth colony, but for the sake of continuity in our story, let's revisit it one more time.

The Pilgrims were considered to be a rather strange sect of people. In fact, they were so misunderstood and so persecuted in their own country, England, they did what they had to do in order to worship God the way they wanted to - they moved. At first, the king of England, James I, was rather antagonistic toward the group, prohibiting them from leaving England and imprisoning them when they tried.

Let's rewind just a bit to connect the dots on some of the history leading up to this point. This king, James I, was the predecessor of Elizabeth I, also known as Good Queen Bess, whom we met in our last chapter. James' mother was Mary, Queen of Scotts, the great niece of that famously crazy king, Henry VIII of England. When Mary, Queen of Scotts, abdicated in order to leave the throne to her young son, James, he also became the distant heir to the throne of England, where his great great uncle's daughters, Mary and Elizabeth, were ruling. (Talk about a confusing family tree!) When Elizabeth I died, leaving no heir of her own, James I became the king of England, while he was still the king of Scotland. King James I was now king of what we call Great Britain.

James I was suspicious of religious groups that did not fit his view of what was acceptable. He was a Protestant, but only to the point of making sure all Catholics understood that the Roman Catholic Pope had no authority over him. Like his ancestors before him, he rebelled against the Italian Pope's authority in England, seeing it as a matter of politics more than religion. When the Pilgrims separated themselves from the Church of England and decided to worship God the way they chose, they attracted the king's attention.

Chapter 2

Eventually, after much persecution and imprisonment, the Pilgrims made their way to Leyden, Holland, and there they stayed for eleven years. While they were in Holland, the Pilgrims worked hard to get their religious literature and fliers back into England, into the hands of their friends and family members, who had remained there. They used flour barrels and potato sacks to smuggle these contraband, religious writings over the water of the English Channel.

> *The Pilgrims used a version of the Bible called the Geneva Bible. This Bible was truly the "people's Bible," with study notes and easier to understand wording. King James of England did not like the fact that the common people had access to a Bible, and therefore, could study it for themselves. This concept challenged his sovereignty and the whole establishment of upper class and royalty.*

As time passed by and the Pilgrims became accustomed to their new life in Holland, the leaders became fearful that the group was losing its identity. Young people were marrying the Dutch, and many in the group were not as focused on their spiritual growth as they used to be. The groups leaders, John Robinson, John Carver, and William Bradford, joined together to decide what to do about this situation. Many of these leaders believed that the answer to their problem lay across the ocean in the New World. It would be hard work, fraught with peril, but they believed that God was calling them to go forth and establish a colony in America - a colony founded on religious freedom.

Let's take a moment here to explore the ways the English financed and organized these New World colonies. You probably realize by now that starting a colony in America was not an easy undertaking. When Sir Walter Raleigh tried to start colonies on Roanoke Island, he lost two times! He invested a tremendous amount of his wealth into these endeavors and ended up with nothing to show for it.

When it became evident that building a lasting colony in America was a risky investment, English investors devised a plan. They began to form joint-stock companies. You might think of these companies, which were set up with the specific purpose of financing New World settlements, as forerunners to our modern-day corporations. These savvy businessmen would pool their money to start these companies, and they would invite others to invest in their company by buying shares of stock in the company. It was a risky business endeavor,

Chapter 2

but whatever money came from the sale of stocks was invested back into the company to finance the building of the colony. Their ultimate hope was to have the colony be a success and eventually make money for the shareholders. One of the major joint-stock companies that financed the building of colonies was the Virginia Company. The king had to be persuaded to give the joint-stock company a charter saying that they could build on a certain tract of land in the New World. The colonies founded in this way were called "charter colonies."

When the Pilgrims finally arrived in America in 1620, their settlement, Plymouth Colony, was a charter colony. Their charter stated that their tract of land was just to the north of Jamestown. However, the howling winds and winter storms caused their ship, the *Mayflower*, to land well to the north of this location. After surviving a two-month long, tremendously stormy passage across the Atlantic, the group was faced with an extremely rough first winter, in which many of them died.

You can visit a replica of the Mayflower near historic Plymouth Colony.

By the Providence of God, the Pilgrims were rescued by an Indian named Squanto. Their new friend taught them how to plant crops that would grow in this soil and to fertilize the crops with dead fish. By the end of the summer, the inhabitants of Plymouth Colony were strong and hale once more. The summer sun, good nutrition, and their new friendship with the Indians made them healthy, strong, and ready for the coming winter.

Despite the hard passage to the New World, the horrible first winter full of sickness and death, and having to build their settlement from the ground up, Plymouth Colony was much more successful than Jamestown. It might have been because Plymouth Colony was settled by whole families, determined to honor God and to make it in this new home, while Jamestown was inhabited by only fortune-seeking men for the first twelve years. Men tend to work harder and better when they know that the people they love most are depending on them.

Chapter 3 — The Colonial Period – Part 2

The settling of Plymouth Colony inspired another religious group, the Puritans, to leave England. Weary of the rising taxes and the persecution of their church, twenty-six Puritan businessmen made the decision to form their own company, the Massachusetts Bay Company. These men desired to establish a colony in America. After receiving a charter from the king, the leaders of the company recruited over a thousand willing participants interested in the company's endeavor.

In 1630, ten years after the founding of Plymouth Colony, seventeen ships arrived in Massachusetts Bay, carrying all of the settlers and the supplies they would need. The settlers joined another group, who had already established a town named Salem. Soon small villages, such as Boston, Watertown, Dorchester, and New Towne (later called Cambridge), which quickly turned into thriving hubs of enterprise, began springing up all around the original settlement.

These Puritan settlements quickly thrived, because the settlers had learned from the mistakes of those who had come to America before them. They made sure that they had doctors, preachers, and craftsmen among them, and they brought enough supplies with them. Another reason these colonies did well was because of the type of government they had. The founding charter company, the Massachusetts Bay Company, consisted of Puritan men, and therefore, they had a say in the establishing of the government.

Not all of the settlers were Puritan - many of them had simply answered the advertisement for being part of starting a new colony in America - but it was the Puritan leaders who built the churches and set up the schools. It was their goal to set up a state established on Biblical principles, one that would be an example for future colonies' governments. The Puritan government was very strict, allowing only church members to vote. The non-church member citizens were allowed to live in the colonies, but they had to adhere to the strict codes of conduct, which allowed the Puritan leaders to control the society.

Chapter 3

Not everyone wanted to listen to the Puritan leaders' ideas about societal control. A pastor in Salem was one of the first who was brave enough to speak up. Roger Williams was a Puritan himself and agreed with their beliefs in general, but he disagreed strongly on three main points.

First, he believed that the government and the church should be separate - not in the way we hear today, however. Mr. Williams believed that the government didn't have a right to enforce a certain belief system onto the citizens. He honestly felt that the Puritans did not have a right to tell all of the colonists what to believe and how to worship God. This did not go over well with the other Puritan leaders, who wanted to be able to rule by their interpretation of the Bible.

The second point of disagreement between Roger Williams and the other Puritan leaders was concerning the Indians. Williams believed that the land, on which the colonists were living, belonged to the Indians. He felt that the colonists should pay the Indians a fair price for the land. The Puritan leaders argued that the king of England had given them this land to settle. English explorers had "found" the land and claimed it for future English settlements which, in their minds, voided them from having to pay for anything.

The final point of contention between Roger Williams and other the Puritan leaders was of a theological nature. Williams sincerely believed that the Puritan leaders were trying to purify the Church of England from within. He believed that the Pilgrims of Plymouth Colony had been correct in completely leaving the church, and he spoke out about the Puritans following their example.

The Puritan leaders brought Roger Williams to trial for voicing these new and "dangerous" opinions. They decided that in order to keep the peace, Roger Williams must go, and thus, they exiled him from their midst. Williams spent a bitterly freezing winter with the Narragansett Indians, who considered him to be an honest and true friend. When the weather broke, and spring brought the warm sun and early leaves, Roger Williams bought a tract of land from the Indians, just south of where he had spent the winter.

Chapter 3

On his newly purchased land, Williams established his own settlement, which he named Providence, in appreciation of the guiding hand and bountiful provision of his Heavenly Father. Providence was established on the firmly held beliefs that had caused Williams to be exiled from Massachusetts. He welcomed all newcomers, regardless of their beliefs, and he was soon joined by some of his friends from his old church in Salem. In 1644, Providence, along with several other settlements, was named the colony of Rhode Island. The colony then drew up a constitution, guaranteeing that the government would have authority in civil matters alone.

New Hampshire and Connecticut joined Massachusetts and Rhode Island to form the New England Colonies. Maine was there also, but because it was governed by Massachusetts, it did not become a separate colony.

As we have learned, the New England Colonies were settled by the English and mostly for religious purposes. Sections of the land south of the New England Colonies had been claimed and partially settled many years before by the Dutch and the Swedes, and by the time England gained control over it, there was an established

Chapter 3

culture already securely in place. These colonies shared the dream of carving out a new type of life from the vast and rough land, and as time passed, their distinct cultures blended into a new culture - American.

New York had originally been explored by an Englishman named Henry Hudson, who had explored for both England and the Netherlands. In 1609, Hudson discovered the river which is now named after him. He was exploring for the Dutch (the Netherlands) at the time, and his exploration gave the Dutch claim to that region. The settlement that they built there, New Netherland, would eventually be taken over by the English and renamed New York for the Duke of York. The Dutch sent settlers in 1624 to settle this area. Some of them settled on Manhattan Island, but most of them went up the river, near to where Albany is now.

In the year 1497, an English explorer named John Cabot had claimed the Atlantic coast of North America for England. The English king gave the Dutch colony to his brother, the Duke of York, who in turn, decided to press England's claim on this land. The duke sent warships to take took control of the area, and the Dutch surrendered without a fight - the colony passed peacefully into the Britain's hands.

New Jersey was founded shortly after this when the Duke of York gave that area to two of his friends, Sir George Carteret and Lord John Berkeley. Pennsylvania was settled by a man named William Penn, who made a monumental agreement with the Indians. His peace treaties with the Native Americans and his philosophy of brotherly love made his colony a huge success. Pennsylvania became one of the most wealthy and the most peaceful of all of the early American colonies. The colony of Delaware was under the governing and protection of Pennsylvania.

The next section of colonies to the south were the Southern Colonies. We have learned about the settling of Jamestown, the first permanent settlement in the colony of Virginia. Jamestown had struggled mightily for the first dozen years of its existence, but with the introduction of a new crop - tobacco - the colony finally turned the corner and started to make a profit for the charter company's shareholders. By the year 1620, the king of England was unhappy with the way Jamestown was being managed and revoked the company's charter, making Jamestown a royal colony. Throughout the the 1600s, towns and

Chapter 3

plantations grew out and around the original colony. One of these towns, Williamsburg, became the capital of the colony toward the end of the century, when a fire destroyed most of Jamestown. Williamsburg went on to become a leader in colonial government.

The colony of Maryland was settled in 1633 by a group of Catholics, who were trying to escape the persecution they were enduring in England. The English king at that time was tolerant of the Catholics and granted them a charter to establish a colony just to the north of Virginia. The colony was named after Queen Henrietta Maria of England. As other religious groups, including a large number of Protestants moved into Maryland, the lawmakers passed the Act of Toleration to protect the Catholics from any potential persecution.

Carolina was settled in the 1660s, primarily by French Huguenots, Scotch-Irish, and English. This colony became wealthy from growing cash crops, such as tobacco, like Jamestown, and indigo, a plant used for a rich, blue dye. In 1712, Carolina split into North Carolina and South Carolina.

Georgia, the most southern colony, was established for two reasons. The first reason was to create a type of "buffer" between the English colonies and the Spanish colony of Florida. The other reason was to provide a more friendly environment for those who found themselves in debtor's prison in England. An English general named James Oglethorpe, who himself was in debt, was given permission to start the colony in 1733. Very few debtors ever came to live in Georgia, but Oglethorpe worked hard to build the colony. He built strong forts along the coast to protect the colonies from Spanish attack, and in 1742, his Georgia militia defeated a Spanish attack against them.

Chapter 4 — The French and Indian War

We have learned about how the English and the French fought over the rights of the waterways in the ocean and how they both settled large tracts of land in America. The French colonists settled along the St. Lawrence and Mississippi Rivers and around the Great Lakes. Their settlements were centered around the fur trade, and the French wanted nothing more than to control this trade throughout North America. You can see on the map below that the English had colonies stretching down the eastern sea coast. Directly "behind" these colonies, to the west, are the Appalachian Mountains, which served as a natural barrier to the rest of the continent. To the west of the mountains, was a strip of land, the Ohio River valley, which both England and France had laid claim to. It was this land, and the rich fishing grounds off of the coast of Newfoundland, that the argument was about.

The French had quite a few advantages in their favor. Their forts were strategically placed along the major rivers and at crucial points throughout the wilderness. The French also enjoyed a powerful friendship with many of the Native Americans, who knew that it was in their best interest to help the French defeat the English and their possible spread over the mountains, into their hunting grounds. Many of the Indian tribes detested the English and were eager to help the French. In spite of their advantages, the French also dealt with one major weakness: they did not have a big American population. In fact, their settlements were so sparsely populated and spread so far apart that it would be difficult to defend all of their forts well at one time.

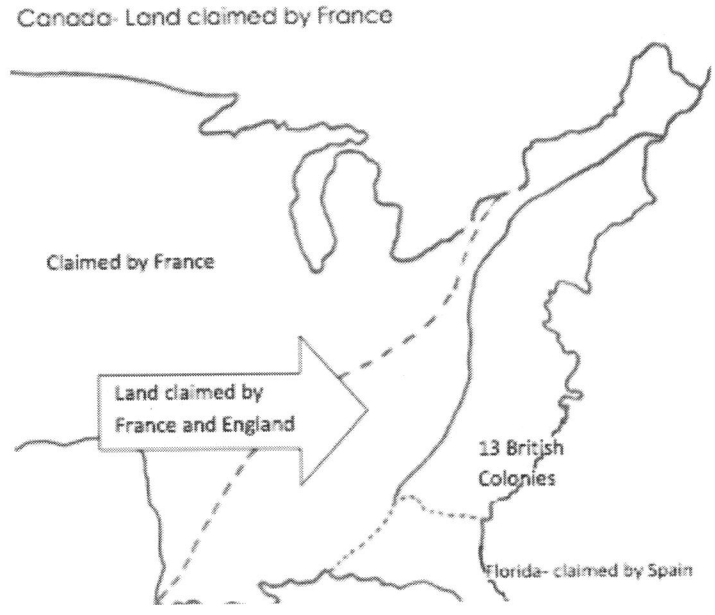

The English had several significant odds in their favor. First and foremost, their population was nearly fifteen times the number of the French. It

Chapter 4

also helped them to know that their navy was the most powerful in the world, and the Iroquois Indian nation, the strongest confederation of Indian Tribes in North America, was on their side. In spite of everything they had in their favor, the English had one major weakness: their lack of unity.

Each of the colonies thought of themselves as a separate entity. They were not one country; they each had their own governing power, their own money, and their own type of society. When the English and the French were fighting, the British American colonies were geographically and politically caught in the middle. Even though the colonies were all ultimately ruled by the British crown, the colonists were the ones living in America - not the king or the parliament - and the outcome of this war would affect them most. It was with great reluctance that most of the American colonists fought this war they had come to call the French and Indian War.

When the war started, the struggle was focused on who would control the Ohio River Valley, where the Allegheny and Monongahela Rivers joined their forces to form the Ohio River (the present location of Pittsburgh, Pennsylvania). The British desired to open this fertile area for settlement, while the French wanted to maintain the control of the trapping industry. The French knew that if the English gained control of this area, it would create an opening for the English to advance further to the west.

In 1754, a group of men from Virginia went to this location with instructions to build a fort, and the governor of Virginia ordered a group of militiamen to go protect them as they built it. (The story of the young officer in charge is the *Focus On: Biography* at the end of this chapter.) The ensuing battle, between this group of militiamen and the French, marked the beginning of the French and Indian War. The French finished the fort that the Virginians had begun and named it Fort Duquesne (doo-CANE).

During the early years of the war, the French successfully drove the English from the Ohio River Valley. The Indians, who were used to fighting in the wilderness, taught the French the tactics that made their smaller numbers unimportant. The British, with their bright red coats, made mighty fine targets for the well-hidden French and Indians! Time after time, the British marched in formation, only to find themselves surrounded by the enemy, dodging

Chapter 4

arrows, and trying to find a target on which to return fire. The Indians and many of the French used bows and arrows, which, in many battles, proved to be a much better weapon than the Englishmen's slow-loading muskets.

I can imagine that the atmosphere in the colonies was rather on edge during this time. Would the Iroquois Indians, who were friendly to the British, continue to sympathize with them? Or would they side with the French, who seemed to be winning this struggle over land and control? Many of the colonists were concerned that if the British lost, there would be a major problem with all of the Indians and the French sweeping into the colonies doing whatever they wanted. It was the needed resolution of this potential problem that led to a meeting being called in June of 1754.

Delegates from several colonies were called to meet in Albany, New York, to discuss what to do. These delegates became known as the Albany Congress, and they met with several of the leaders of the Iroquois Nation to support the British in the war. This meeting was important for another reason as well; the Albany Congress developed a plan of union to submit to the colonies. The Albany Plan of Union was primarily brought about by Benjamin Franklin. It stated that the colonies were not strong - separated and independent like they were - but if they would unite as one, they would become stronger and be able to stand against the French. This plan of union was not accepted by the colonies. Each one feared that by giving up their own independence to become part of a larger union of colonies, they would eventually lose their freedom and strength. As the French and the Indians pushed the British further east, it looked as though the British were fighting a losing battle. In a desperate attempt to regain some foothold in the west, the British decided to march on and capture Fort Duquesne.

British General Edward Braddock, fifteen hundred British soldiers, and approximately one thousand colonial militiamen marched northward toward the French fort. Among the militiamen was our friend, George Washington, who had been assigned to be aide-de-camp to General Braddock. As the men marched slowly toward their destination, they cleared roads and built bridges. Although Washington tried to warn his superior officer of the dangers in the wilderness, Braddock would not listen. Before the British forces had reached Fort

Chapter 4

Duquesne, the French were well aware of their approach and were prepared to give their enemy quite a thrashing. General Braddock was fatally wounded, and it was his young aide-de-camp who was responsible for getting the remaining troops home to safety. The death of the general and the defeat at Fort Duquesne left the English American colonies feeling more defeated than ever.

It wasn't until 1756 that the British war effort started turning around. The British army stationed in America and the war effort was handed over to a new and much more energetic general; William Pitt was just who the British needed! He took the discouraged American colonists and their scattered militia groups and brought them together, turning their half-hearted efforts into an aggressive war campaign. Pitt scouted around looking for talented, young generals in the colonies for the British army. He required the militia and the army to fight together as a united front, giving the colonists any training they needed to be able to fight well.

With his newly energized, equipped, and trained forces, Pitt strategically began attacking pivotal French forts and locations. One by one, the French lost their forts to the British. In late 1758, British forces took over Fort Duquesne, rebuilding the badly-damaged fort and renaming it after their much-admired leader; Fort Pitt became a symbol of hope for the American colonies.

William Pitt then turned his attention on Quebec; he knew that if he could capture this important fort, he would have the French. Taking Quebec would not be easy, however, because the placement of the well-fortified fort was absolutely ideal for keeping out any outside attackers. Fort Quebec, situated high above the St. Lawrence River, was protected by high cliffs and seemed invincible.

The British, under the command of General James Wolfe, tried unsuccessfully to conquer the fort by laying siege, but the inhabitants simply waited them out. This happened several times until General Wolfe decided on a daring move. Under the cover of the dark one night, General Wolfe and his troops, silently crossed the river downstream of the fort, and like so many ants, thay swarmed up the side of the cliffs. By morning, four thousand British troops had positioned themselves in battle position on a plain a short distance from

Chapter 4

the fort. When the French awoke the next morning, they could not have been more shocked, for there, right in their own "back yard" were the British ready to attack them!

The battle that ensued ended in a British victory even though both the British general, James Wolfe, and the French commander, Marquis de Montcalm, were both slain. The French surrendered Quebec to the British that day. A year later, Montreal also fell to the British, and the war was over. The Peace of Paris was negotiated. France gave up any lands east of the Mississippi River except New Orleans, and Canada went under British rule. Britain emerged from the war as the strongest nation in the world.

Focus On: Biography - Young George Washington

Twenty-one year old George Washington was a hero of the French and Indian War. Raised from a young age to work hard, study hard, and honor those in authority, George was the model young officer. In this chapter, we learned about two battles in which young George Washington played a part. Interestingly, both of these battles, although important for many reasons, did not end victoriously for George Washington or the British.

When George Washington and his men marched to protect the Virginians building the fort in the Ohio River Valley, he did not know that the approaching battle with the French would be the most important event in his young life so far. As they marched along toward the fort, Washington and his men fought and defeated a small French force. From these men, Washington learned that there was a much larger and stronger French regiment nearby. George Washington and his men retreated and hastily built a stockade in which to protect themselves from what they knew was coming. This stockade was called Fort Necessity. Washington and his men must have impressed the French commanders. Even though they had beaten this small group of Virginia militiamen and their young officer in charge, the French allowed the colonists to return to Virginia.

Chapter 4

Several years later, George Washington was assigned to be the rather pompous General Braddock's aide-de-camp. As the British troops marched on Fort Duquesne, the French and Indians were suddenly everywhere. Arrows rained down on the unprepared British. Washington had tried to warn the British general that the Indians and French did not fight in the same way that the British had been taught; they used their natural surroundings - the trees, rocks, and grass - as part of both their defense and offense. General Braddock would hear nothing of it. He was a highly trained, professional soldier who would not think of lowering himself to fight from behind a tree or a rock!

As the fighting ensued and General Braddock was wounded, Washington rode his horse back and forth, encouraging the men and giving orders during the battle. Washington's bravery during this battle became legendary. There are reports of how he had bullet holes in his clothing and hat, yet not a hair of his head was hurt. He had three horses shot out from under him, yet he came away unscathed.

An Indian warrior, who witnessed Washington's behavior that day, talked to George Washington and his friend, Dr. James Craik, fifteen years after that battle. Washington and Craik had returned to those same Pennsylvania woods where the famous battle had taken place. This is what the old Indian warrior said:

"I have traveled a long and weary path that I might see the young warrior of the great battle...I am come to pay homage to the man who is the particular favorite of Heaven, and who can never die in battle."

There have been books written about this battle and how it seems to many that George Washington was indeed protected by Heaven.

The Revolutionary Period

1763 - 1787

Chapter 5: Rebellion Against Tyranny and Oppression

Chapter 6: The Revolutionary War: Part 1

Chapter 7: The Revolutionary War: Part 2

Chapter 8: The Treaty of Paris and the Confederation of the Colonies

Please leave blank.

Chapter 5 — Rebellion Against Tyranny and Oppression

The French and Indian War had ended in the British victory, making the British empire the strongest and most influential in the world. As the British empire grew, the government tightened control - especially in the colonies. There were hard feelings between the British government and many of the American colonies. Britain was perturbed because of the American colonies' half-hearted support during the French and Indian War. Certain members of the British parliament were convinced that the American colonies had been given too much independence and freedom, and many in parliament viewed the colonies as children who had become wise in their own eyes. As a result, the British sent more troops to the colonies to patrol and enforce the laws and taxes. The American colonists were expected to house and feed the troops while they were here in America. This demand did nothing to help the hard feelings, as the soldiers consumed the colonists' hard-earned income. For the most part, all of these British troops were not welcome.

The British government also set laws into place, which declared that the colonists could not settle any further west than the Appalachian Mountains. These laws were meant to squelch any Indian uprising against the British forts situated in the west. The colonies resented the British presence in their lives; they had always been allowed to govern themselves, and now it seemed that they were being held captive by their own mother country. Anxiety and resentment grew by leaps and bounds as many of the Americans demanded to know why they were not receiving the same rights as the other British citizens.

So what exactly were these rights that the American colonists were demanding? To better understand this, we need to travel back to England to learn about their type of government...

Many years before our American colonists friends rebelled against the oppressive rule of Britain, England herself was struggling at the hands of a tyrannical, egotistical king. If you are familiar with the story of the Middle Ages, you have no doubt heard the story of the

Chapter 5

good king, Richard the Lionhearted. Richard was followed by his younger brother, John Lackland (named after the fact that he did not have large holdings of land).

Brother John became King John and proceeded to become known as one of the very worst kings in the history of England. As the story goes, John was so awful and so hard to deal with that his officials and lords captured him and demanded that he sign an agreement stating that he - and all of the following monarchs of England - did not have the right to do whatever they felt like doing. This event, which took place in 1215, became one of the most important events in world history. This agreement, the Magna Carta, marked the end of accepted tyrannical rule. It stated that the king or queen had to follow the same laws that everyone else did.

I suppose the American rebellion eventually would have happened no matter what, considering the independent nature of most of the colonists. After all, it was this stubborn independence that enabled them to successfully carve whole towns, cities, and entire colonies out of the raw wilderness. As the situation worsened, whispers of breaking away from England began to blow like a breeze throughout the colonies.

Benjamin Franklin - we can always count on him for some good-natured humor - wrote this about the mother country...

"We have an old mother that peevish is grown,

She snubs us like children that scarce walk alone.

She forgets we're grown up and sense of our own." B. Franklin

Chapter 5

The king, George III, was on the throne in England. He had never been to America, and neither had many of his parliament. They simply wanted the colonists to obey orders and do what they were told. The king and the parliament decided to implement a plan to teach the wayward colonists a lesson. This plan included taxes that were especially for the American colonies.

King George was not known to be exceptionally politically savvy. He was, instead, very stubborn and self-centered. When he levied taxes and the colonists screamed, he just stomped his foot and demanded obedience. The more taxes he imposed, the angrier the Americans became; the angrier they became, the more they boycotted the taxed items.

Boycotting the taxed items was rather difficult to say the least, because these were the goods of everyday life. Sugar, molasses, wine, coffee, herbs, silks, and linens were the first to be taxed in 1764. This tax was called the Sugar Act. The Stamp Act followed in 1765. This tax was on all legal documents, envelopes, newspapers, and even playing cards. In 1767, the Townshend Acts taxed lead, glass, paint, and tea.

As the Americans dealt with the oppression of the unfair treatment, they thought of their rights as Englishmen. Didn't they deserve to be treated with the same respect and freedom as their fellow Englishmen living in England? As in all situations like this, people started taking sides. Those who supported the British actions and felt that the colonies should submit to the British rules and taxes were called "Tories." The colonials who believed that Britain did not have a right to enforce these taxes and rules on the American colonies were called "Patriots." Division of this sort is never easy; families were divided by these differing loyalties, which only added to the atmosphere of impending doom.

On March 5, 1770, emotions reached a feverish pitch as four hundred colonists gathered in the Boston streets. An argument between a British officer and a wigmaker had escalated out of control, and the angry throng began throwing snowballs at the soldiers, who were trying to assist the British officer. The troops fired into the crowd, and when the smoke cleared, three colonists lay dead and two more were severely wounded. This incident became known as the Boston Massacre.

Chapter 5

Boston was one of the busiest seaports in the colonies, with commercial ships clogging its ports. At the time of the Boston Massacre, there were approximately sixteen thousand inhabitants in the city, making it one of the largest cities in America. Boston also had several outstanding churches, universities, and libraries. Many great minds of the era came from Boston, including Samuel Adams, John Hancock, a city official, John Adams, and a silversmith and printer named Paul Revere. These would be some of the heroes of the fight for freedom.

After the Boston Massacre, the British Parliament repealed some of the taxes, and the atmosphere in the colonies calmed down somewhat. However, in 1773, a new tax on tea brought an abrupt end to the calm. On December 16, 1773, a group of Patriots dressed as Indians stormed aboard a British cargo ship bobbing in the Boston Harbor and carrying hundreds of boxes of tea. Once on board the ship, the Patriots chopped open the boxes and dumped hundreds and hundreds of pounds of tea into the icy water.

When King George heard about this wildly rebellious tea party, he became irate. As a punishment, he enacted the Intolerable Acts, which closed the colonies' harbors to all shipping, restricted town meetings, and increased the number of troops stationed in America. Life was looking grim for the colonists, but behind closed doors, secret meetings were taking place. Men from all walks of life were coming forward to voice their opinions about the future of America. Most of them believed that it would take fighting England to gain independence and freedom.

These meetings were led by leading patriots, who called themselves "The Sons of Liberty." Cousins John and Samuel Adams believed that America could govern themselves.

Chapter 5

They wanted the colonies to have the chance to unite under a central government. The idea of a government run by the people, for the people was something new - a novel idea, which wasn't being thought about in most of the world. Could men be trusted to govern themselves? Could they wisely choose their own leaders?

At this time in our history, many pamphlets, newsletters, and newspaper articles were being written and published, outlining British policies concerning the American colonies. Of course, there were no swift ways of communication in those days, so there had to be a network of trusted messengers to convey the messages as speedily as possible to the general public. Samuel Adams is credited most for establishing this first organized committee to spread the word quickly.

Samuel Adams' Committees of Correspondence consisted of political leaders from all of the colonies, and it was this committee that became the First Continental Congress. This new Continental Congress met in Philadelphia, Colonial America's leading city, to discuss what they should do. Representatives came from every colony except Georgia.

Samuel and John Adams were both there, representing Massachusetts. New York representatives, Alexander McDougall and John Jay, came to suggest that the colonies put pressure on England by refusing to receive her imported goods. (We will learn more about this interesting fellow later!) John Dickson, from Philadelphia, believed that there *had* to be a way to get along with England, while Christopher Gadsden from South Carolina and Patrick Henry from Virginia disagreed loudly with this notion. The Congress managed to pass ten resolutions listing the rights of the colonists, and they wrote an agreeable and respectful letter to King George, asking him to consider their complaints.

Focus On: Biography – **Benjamin Franklin**

Benjamin was born in Boston, in 1706, one of seventeen children, ten of which were boys. Ben was the youngest son, and he went to formal school for only two years before he had to come home to help his family. His father was a candle maker and a soap maker, and he needed help running his shop, but Benjamin did not like making candles and soap. Nevertheless, he worked hard dipping candles and stirring the tallow for the soap. Benjamin

Chapter 5

was an extremely intelligent and imaginative boy, who daydreamed of having adventures at sea.

When he was twelve, Ben's father sent him to work for his older brother, James, as an apprentice. Benjamin's brother was a printer and owned his own shop. Ben and his brother did not get along very well. Benjamin liked being a printer, but he did not like the fact that he had to work without pay for nine years, until he was twenty-one years old.

Ben decided that he was going to learn how to write well, so that he would have a fine education by the time he was free from his apprenticeship. He could not go to school, so Ben came up with a plan. To accomplish his goal, he read articles, speeches, and documents. After thinking about what he had read for several days, he would write what he had read from memory. After he was satisfied with his writing, he would very carefully compare and correct his work against the original. Benjamin became an exceptionally good writer in this way.

Benjamin's brother started a newspaper called the New England Courant, and Benjamin worked for him. He learned how to edit, set type, and run the printing presses. Ben thought the articles and advertisements were fascinating. In fact, he thought they were so interesting that he decided to write some articles of his own. Ben, knowing that his brother would not print something that he had written, wrote his article the way he wanted and signed his name "Silence Dogood." The articles poked fun at the Puritan Church for being so strict, and most people thought they were funny, so he wrote thirteen more. Ben enjoyed writing for the newspaper and making people laugh and think.

Not everyone in Boston was laughing at his articles, though, and his brother got into trouble for printing articles poking fun at the Puritan Church. He was told that he could not run his printing shop anymore, so he made Ben run it instead. Benjamin enjoyed being the editor of his brother's newspaper, but this change did not help his relationship with his brother.

After his apprenticeship, Ben decided to go look for a job in another printing shop, so he left Boston and went to Philadelphia, the City of Brotherly Love. Ben loved Philadelphia,

Chapter 5

and always considered it his home town. He spent many years working in a printing shop, and eventually, he owned his own.

Ben was becoming a very well known character throughout the colonies. People liked him for his charming smile, and his quick wittiness made them think. He was always coming up with riddles and sayings...

"Early to bed, early to rise, makes a man healthy, wealthy and wise" or "A penny saved is a penny earned"

Ben was so well-known for his witty comments that he wrote a book called "Poor Richard's Almanac," which was extremely popular throughout the Colonies. This book was not only full of humor; it also predicted the weather and told farmers when it would be best to plant their crops.

Eventually, Benjamin married a lady named Deborah, and they had three children. He loved his family and spent hours playing with his children, and he commonly referred to Deborah as "my beloved wife."

Besides writing books and starting the Postal Service, Ben was also an inventor. He loved science and was very curious by nature. Ben wasn't satisfied with knowing that something worked; he wanted to know WHY it worked. He also wanted to invent things that made life easier for people - like bifocal glasses, lightning rods to keep houses safer during lightning storms, and a stove that was more efficient and warmer. Benjamin was also the very first United States PostMaster, deciding to make life easier by organizing a more efficient method of delivering the mail.

Also among Ben Franklin's interests were politics and abolition. When the colonies were struggling under England's ever-tightening grasp, Ben wanted to help. By this time, he was getting on in age and knew that he couldn't be on the frontlines fighting to help his beloved America. At first, Benjamin thought that he could help by trying to bring peace between the colonies and their mother country. He did not believe that England was truly trying to harm

Chapter 5

them; they just didn't understand what it meant to be American. This is when Franklin decided to become a diplomat. When the situation deteriorated past the point of repair, Franklin came home to help his fellow American leaders to come up with the best plan of action. He was sent to several European countries to employ his wise words, to secure help and ammunition for the Patriots.

Ben Franklin is one of the most well known and well loved of all of the Founding Fathers. His ingenuity and independent nature exemplify the American spirit. His contributions to the country's struggle for independence are monumental.

Chapter 6
The Revolutionary War: Part 1
Give Me Liberty or Give Me Death

The next period of American history gallops onto the scene, accompanied by the wild tempo of the beat of a horse's hooves. Henry Wadsworth Longfellow's epic poem, *The Ride of Paul Revere,* tells the story of the fateful night before the dawn of the Revolutionary War. Although we are most familiar with the ride of Paul Revere, there were two other men, William Dawes and Dr. Samuel Prescott, who also bravely flew through the dark of night crying out the alarm... *"The British are coming! The British are coming!"*

But wait, I'm getting ahead of myself. Let me back up a bit to fill in the backdrop for this fateful night that so famously prefaced the dawn of the War for Independence.

Even though England's grip on the colonies had become a suffocating stranglehold, some of the colonists believed they could and should talk out their differences with their mother country - these folks were called Loyalists. War was not even an option for these colonial citizens; after all, Britain was distinctively the most powerful nation on the earth at the time. Many thought it would be not only completely futile to fight them, but also potentially suicidal. This talk of war was treason, and the consequences of a failed attempt to gain freedom... well, it was not a pleasant thought!

Other colonists were convinced that it would take fighting to bring peace. Even though it seemed that Britain had all of the odds stacked in her favor, these patriots were willing to pay the price for the freedom they so desperately yearned for. It was with the realization that they must prepare for the worst that these brave men started to stockpile weapons and munitions. Cannonballs and gunpowder began to pile up in the town of Concord, a town about twenty miles from Boston, as the great network of colonial militia, the MinuteMen, readied themselves for the signal to fight.

All over the colonies, a tremendous spy ring remained alert for any indication of when or where the British would make their move. Nerves were taut, and emotions were running high. The Sons of Liberty, with the cousins, John and Samuel Adams, at their lead, waited to hear word of the British troops' movements. Paul Revere, a silversmith from the city of

Chapter 6

Boston, had become more keenly and personally interested in the political climate of the colonies when the British taxes and sanctions affected his business. Revere became one of the more outspoken Patriots of Boston and was keenly aware of the rumors filtering through the spy network - the British were planning an attack. Which way were they coming - by land or by sea? Revere was concerned for his friends, Sam Adams and John Hancock, who were hiding in Lexington, a town near Concord and the hidden munitions.

Paul Revere spoke with Robert Newman, the sexton of the Old North Church in Boston. The two agreed upon a signal, lanterns hung high in the church's steeple, which would tell Revere and the other riders which way the British were coming - one if by land, two if by sea. Breathlessly, Revere silently rowed across the Charlestown River, passing like a shadow under the very nose of the British, onboard a huge frigate anchored in the bay. Upon reaching the far shore, Revere turned, his eyes searching the horizon for the signal. There! Two twinkling lights cut through the darkness of night. "They are coming by sea!" came the message silently and swiftly. Revere swung into the saddle, his Patriot friends solemnly waved as he pointed the horse's head toward the northwest, toward Lexington and Concord...

The following morning, the first shot of the Revolutionary War rang out. This would become known in history as "the shot heard around the world."

* * * * * * * *The Three Firebrands* * * * * * * * * *

In this chapter, we are going to take a look at three men who would become known throughout history as "the three firebrands." A firebrand is a stick of slow-burning wood with a spark on the end. This stick with the glowing spark at its end is used to start a fire in a tinderbox, fireplace, or wood stove and may be compared to a modern, fireplace match. These three men, Samuel Adams, Patrick Henry, and Thomas Paine were all instrumental in the beginning days of the fight for freedom. Thomas Paine was a great writer, Patrick Henry was a gifted orator, and Samuel Adams was mostly gifted at stirring people up.

These three men were exactly what the colonists needed at this point in history. It would take the colonies a long time to consider themselves to be one country. Benjamin Franklin had drawn what is considered to be the first political cartoon in American history in

Chapter 6

1754, when the colonies sent representatives to discuss what to do about the French and Indian war. As you can see, it was Mr. Franklin's opinion that the division between the colonies would eventually lead to their ruin, if they did not join together and fight. In 1754, the colonies were not ready to give up their own independent identities to become one nation under one name. By the 1770s, however, it was becoming clear that the cut up snake was going to have to combine its efforts and allegiance to survive. The three firebrands helped them to do this.

Focus On: Biography #1 - Samuel Adams

Samuel Adams was born in September of 1722 and was raised in a strict Puritan home, an influence that long evidenced itself in his life's moral code. Young Samuel went to Harvard College, where he graduated as a businessman, but that was never his passion. As we learned in our last chapter, Samuel is credited for establishing the Committees of Correspondence to help unite the colonies by spreading the news of the political happenings.

Sam smiled as he watched prominent groups of citizens in various colonies writing back and forth to each other, working together to find solutions to their common problems and sending their messages through his Committees of Correspondence. Sam also started other groups; one of these was the Sons of Liberty. In Boston, the group met under an old elm tree, which Sam Adams called the Liberty Tree. Of course, the British chopped that tree down as soon as they realized what was going on, but that didn't stop the Sons of Liberty.

Chapter 6

Although Samuel Adams was a political genius, he was not exceptionally business savvy; he was always broke and wearing rather shabby and wrinkled clothing, because his mind was always consumed with the political temperature in the colonies. Sam's appearance did not tell you what kind of fellow he truly was, but his fingers were constantly positioned over the pulse of life around him. His rabble-rousing and agitating angered the British so much that they declared him to be a public enemy, an outlaw, and a troublemaker. It seems that the British knew what Samuel was truly up to! They knew he wanted the colonies to not only earn their independence; he also wanted America to be a grand and wonderful country, one that was completely unique and completely free of kings, queens, and royally pampered blue-bloods.

Samuel was a visionary, thoroughly versed in the history of the Pilgrims, the Puritans, and the Quakers, who came to America for freedom. He wanted America to be the first country in the history of the world where the PEOPLE governed themselves. His vision saw into what he hoped would be the future of the land he loved so much.

 *Focus On: Biography #2* - **Thomas Paine**

Our next of the three firebrands is a young Englishman, who has been called "a corsetmaker by trade, a journalist by profession, and a propagandist by inclination." Unlike Sam Adams, Tom Paine was not born in America. In fact, he had not been in the colonies long at all when he became an American Patriot. As a boy in England, he had been an apprentice to a corsetmaker. (Now there's an illustrious career for you!) Thomas did not like his job at the corsetmaker's shop, so he ran away and went to sea. After a brief and unsuccessful stint at sea, Tom tried his hand at being a grocer, a teacher, and a tobacco salesman. None of these potential career paths excited

Chapter 6

Thomas, but it was during this time that he met Benjamin Franklin, while the elderly statesman was visiting London on one of his diplomatic trips. Thomas knew that he wanted to go to America, and Dr. Franklin gave him a letter that would give him a job as a writer and editor at a magazine in Philadelphia.

On the voyage to America, Paine became extremely ill with a fever and almost died. When he arrived in America, he had to be carried ashore. Tom was young and strong, though, and before long, he was up and working at his new job. His words flowed in such an impressive way that the readers took notice. Thomas had finally found the perfect job. As Thomas became accustomed to living in America, he became more and more aware of the political unrest. He saw that the colonies were pulling away from their mother country, and he heard the murmuring and contemplations about whether what they were doing was right or not. Thomas thought about this and then wrote a little book.

Tom's book was titled *Common Sense*, and in it, he clearly articulated what the people already knew to be true. He outlined these three important concepts: monarchy is a constrictive and harsh form of government, and the colonies did not need that type of oppressive rule over them; the taxes being levied against the colonies were unfair and tyrannical, and they were hurting the colonies economy; it was ridiculous for a small island-nation, which was 3,000 miles away - across an ocean - to try to rule an entire, huge continent.

When *Common Sense* rolled off of the printing presses and were passed into the hands of the colonists, America nodded its collective head - yes, it was common sense. Britain did not have a right to oppress them. *Common Sense* immediately became a top-seller, and Thomas Paine became a well-known Patriot. His words stirred the hearts of his new countrymen.

Focus On: Biography #3 - **Patrick Henry**

"Give me liberty or give me death!" These might be familiar words, but they are not the only ones spoken by Patrick Henry, our third of the three firebrands. Patrick was born

Chapter 6

and raised on a farm in the Virginia frontier. His father was a Scottish immigrant and college graduate, and he taught his son the love of words. Young Patrick learned English and Latin, as he and his father read the Bible together. Patrick loved how the words of the English language flowed like music, and he worked hard to learn to speak well. Patrick was also known for loving a good party; he loved to dance, fiddle, and socialize.

Like Samuel Adams and Thomas Paine, Patrick was not successful at business at the beginning of his life. It seemed that he was trying the wrong occupation - storekeeping first, followed by being a planter. Young Patrick enjoyed life too much to remain in a dreary occupation. His love of a challenge eventually drove him to study law. From there, he entered politics and was elected to the House of Burgesses, which held meetings in Williamsburg, Virginia.

Patrick was serving in the House of Burgesses when the Stamp Act was passed, and he created quite a stir among the older members of the House when he spoke out loudly against what was going on. His speech against the Stamp Act garnered a lot of attention from many people, including a young lawyer named Thomas Jefferson, who thought what Patrick said was ingenious. Not everyone liked what Patrick said, though, and soon the English governor of Virginia became so irate, he dissolved the House of Burgesses.

The members of the House of Burgesses did not disband, however, and Patrick went right on speaking out against the British tyranny. A decade passed, and finally it became too dangerous for the group to meet at their usual gathering place, the Raleigh Tavern. Patrick's most famous speech was delivered in a church in Richmond, Virginia. The crowd gathered there held their breath as Patrick took the floor. He stood there, with his head bowed low, his arms held in front of him as if they were bound with the heaviest of shackles. His words started so quietly, his audience leaned forward to hear, but as he continued, Patrick's voice rose louder and louder, until the walls of the building shuddered...

Chapter 6

"Mr. President, no man thinks more highly than I do of the patriotism, as well as abilities, of the very worthy gentlemen who have just addressed the House. But different men often see the same subject in different lights; and, therefore, I hope it will not be thought disrespectful to those gentlemen if, entertaining as I do, opinions of a character very opposite to theirs, I shall speak forth my sentiments freely, and without reserve. This is no time for ceremony. The question before the House is one of awful moment to this country. For my own part, I consider it as nothing less than a question of freedom or slavery; and in proportion to the magnitude of the subject ought to be the freedom of the debate. It is only in this way that we can hope to arrive at truth, and fulfill the great responsibility which we hold to God and our country. Should I keep back my opinions at such a time, through fear of giving offense, I should consider myself as guilty of treason towards my country, and of an act of disloyalty toward the majesty of heaven, which I revere above all earthly kings.

Mr. President, it is natural to man to indulge in the illusions of hope. We are apt to shut our eyes against a painful truth, and listen to the song of that siren till she transforms us into beasts. Is this the part of wise men, engaged in a great and arduous struggle for liberty? Are we disposed to be of the number of those who, having eyes, see not, and, having ears, hear not, the things which so nearly concern their temporal salvation? For my part, whatever anguish of spirit it may cost, I am willing to know the whole truth; to know the worst, and to provide for it.

I have but one lamp by which my feet are guided; and that is the lamp of experience. I know of no way of judging of the future but by the past. And judging by the past, I wish to know what there has been in the conduct of the British ministry for the last ten years, to justify those hopes with which gentlemen have been pleased to solace themselves, and the House? Is it that insidious smile with which our petition has been lately received? Trust it not, sir; it will prove a snare to your feet. Suffer not yourselves to be betrayed with a kiss. Ask yourselves how this gracious reception of our petition comports with these war-like preparations which cover our waters and darken our land. Are fleets and armies necessary to a work of love and reconciliation? Have we shown ourselves so unwilling to be reconciled, that force must be called in to win back our love? Let us not deceive ourselves, sir. These are the implements of

Chapter 6

war and subjugation; the last arguments to which kings resort. I ask, gentlemen, sir, what means this martial array, if its purpose be not to force us to submission? Can gentlemen assign any other possible motive for it? Has Great Britain any enemy, in this quarter of the world, to call for all this accumulation of navies and armies? No, sir, she has none. They are meant for us; they can be meant for no other. They are sent over to bind and rivet upon us those chains which the British ministry have been so long forging. And what have we to oppose to them? Shall we try argument? Sir, we have been trying that for the last ten years. Have we anything new to offer upon the subject? Nothing. We have held the subject up in every light of which it is capable; but it has been all in vain. Shall we resort to entreaty and humble supplication? What terms shall we find which have not been already exhausted? Let us not, I beseech you, sir, deceive ourselves. Sir, we have done everything that could be done, to avert the storm which is now coming on. We have petitioned; we have remonstrated; we have supplicated; we have prostrated ourselves before the throne, and have implored its interposition to arrest the tyrannical hands of the ministry and Parliament. Our petitions have been slighted; our remonstrances have produced additional violence and insult; our supplications have been disregarded; and we have been spurned, with contempt, from the foot of the throne. In vain, after these things, may we indulge the fond hope of peace and reconciliation. There is no longer any room for hope. If we wish to be free, if we mean to preserve inviolate those inestimable privileges for which we have been so long contending, if we mean not basely to abandon the noble struggle in which we have been so long engaged, and which we have pledged ourselves never to abandon until the glorious object of our contest shall be obtained, we must fight! I repeat it, sir, we must fight! An appeal to arms and to the God of Hosts is all that is left us!

They tell us, sir, that we are weak; unable to cope with so formidable an adversary. But when shall we be stronger? Will it be the next week, or the next year? Will it be when we are totally disarmed, and when a British guard shall be stationed in every house? Shall we gather strength by irresolution and inaction? Shall we acquire the means of effectual resistance, by lying supinely on our backs, and hugging the delusive phantom of hope, until our enemies shall have bound us hand and foot? Sir, we are not weak if we make a proper use of those means which the God of nature hath placed in our power. Three millions of people, armed in

Chapter 6

the holy cause of liberty, and in such a country as that which we possess, are invincible by any force which our enemy can send against us. Besides, sir, we shall not fight our battles alone. There is a just God who presides over the destinies of nations; and who will raise up friends to fight our battles for us. The battle, sir, is not to the strong alone; it is to the vigilant, the active, the brave. Besides, sir, we have no election. If we were base enough to desire it, it is now too late to retire from the contest. There is no retreat but in submission and slavery! Our chains are forged! Their clanking may be heard on the plains of Boston! The war is inevitable and let it come! I repeat it, sir, let it come.

It is in vain, sir, to extenuate the matter. Gentlemen may cry, Peace, Peace! but there is no peace. The war is actually begun! The next gale that sweeps from the north will bring to our ears the clash of resounding arms! Our brethren are already in the field! Why stand we here idle? What is it that gentlemen wish? What would they have? Is life so dear, or peace so sweet, as to be purchased at the price of chains and slavery? Forbid it, Almighty God! I know not what course others may take; but as for me, give me liberty or give me death!"

Chapter 7

The Revolutionary War: Part 2
"These Are Times that Try Men's Souls"

Section 1:

The incidents at Concord and Lexington angered many Americans. Most colonists believed that they would have to fight, but there were still those who did not think the fighting would be for independence from Britain. They believed that they would have to fight to make England listen to their complaints as Englishmen. On May 10, 1775, the Second Continental Congress convened in Philadelphia to discuss what should be done next. The gathered men decided to send a letter to the king asking him to preserve their rights as Englishmen. This petition became known as the Olive Branch Petition.

Although the Congress sent this letter, they were not optimistic of the outcome, and they continued to prepare for war. The army continued to gather at Boston, and the new Commander-in-Chief was named. George Washington came from his home at Mount Vernon, ready to step into the role of the highest ranking army official in the colonies. Colonists from all over America sent provisions and weapons. The atmosphere was solemn; a storm was coming.

As was expected, the king refused the Olive Branch Petition. Instead, he ordered the army to clamp down harder on the rebellious colonies and stated that there would be peace only if they were willing to submit. This act was followed closely by the Prohibitory Act, which cut off British trade with the colonies. Under this act, American ships were subject to capture; Britain no longer would protect them. All of this stubborn tyranny on the king's part angered the colonists. (You researched and wrote about the capture of Fort Ticonderoga and the Battle of Bunker Hill in our last chapter. These events took place following the king's refusal to accept the Olive Branch Petition.)

The British response to the colonies' early military strategies was quick and decisive. They ordered a blockade in New England to keep weapons and supplies from passing back and forth between the colonies. They also hired thousands of mercenaries to help them

Chapter 7

fight. These hired soldiers, called Hessians, were from Germany, and most of them did not even speak English.

When the Americans tried to capture key Canadian cities to keep the British from attacking from the north, the results were rather dismal. Sickness and botched attacks marked the early colonial war efforts. The officers in charge of this campaign, Philip Schuyler, Richard Montgomery, and Benedict Arnold, were not spared this disaster. Schuyler became extremely ill, Montgomery, who was called in to replace Schuyler, was killed, and Arnold was severely wounded.

It was during this time that Thomas Paine wrote a second pamphlet, a series of articles, called *The American Crisis*. This little book was read to the American troops on December 10, 1776, and it rallied the men amid their hardship to rise and prove that they were not "summer soldiers" or "sunshine patriots."

> *December 23, 1776*
> *"THESE are the times that try men's souls. The summer soldier and the sunshine patriot will, in this crisis, shrink from the service of their country; but he that stands by it now, deserves the love and thanks of man and woman. Tyranny, like hell, is not easily conquered; yet we have this consolation with us, that the harder the conflict, the more glorious the triumph. What we obtain too cheap, we esteem too lightly: it is dearness only that gives every thing its value. Heaven knows how to put a proper price upon its goods; and it would be strange indeed if so celestial an article as FREEDOM should not be highly rated. Britain, with an army to enforce her tyranny, has declared that she has a right (not only to TAX) but "to BIND us in ALL CASES WHATSOEVER" and if being bound in that manner, is not slavery, then is there not such a thing as slavery upon earth. Even the expression is impious; for so unlimited a power can belong only to God."*
>   Thomas Paine
> *"The American Crisis"*

During the winter of 1775-1776, the American war effort centered around the goal of removing the British from Boston. One of the most amazing and heroic events of the Revolutionary War occurred during this long winter. A twenty-five-year-old bookseller-turned-soldier from Boston, Colonel Knox, accomplished an almost unbelievable feat of transporting sixty tons of artillery (cannons and ammunition) on forty-two sledges, pulled by eighty teams of oxen, from Fort Ticonderoga to Boston. Through the mountains, snow, and ice, these men battled the elements to bring the precious artillery the three hundred miles to their destination.

Chapter 7

> **F.Y.I.** After reading through Thomas Jefferson's rough draft of the Declaration of Independence, Benjamin Franklin improved Jefferson's phrase "we hold these truths to be sacred and undeniable" to "we hold these truths to be self-evident."

On March 1, the Americans placed the artillery on Dorchester Heights, overlooking Boston. The British army inside of Boston awoke in the morning to see the cannons aimed at the city. The British evacuated the city, sailing south to New York. Over a thousand Loyalists also left Boston at this time, making their way north to settle in Nova Scotia.

It was also during the fall and winter of 1775-1776 that the Continental Congress took decisive steps toward declaring independence from Britain. They created an American navy, which mostly consisted of refurbished merchants' ships and a rather odd selection of other boats and ships. The Congress also purchased more war supplies and made an unofficial acceptance of French aid.

On May 15, the House of Burgesses of Virginia endorsed a resolution for independence. A committee of five men were appointed to write a declaration of independence from Britain. Other committees were also formed to deal with issues of government, including forming a confederation or union and the considerations of foreign alliances. All of these delegations voted for the Declaration, which was written primarily by Thomas Jefferson. On July 4, 1776, the Congress unanimously approved the Declaration of Independence. Fifty-five men signed the document, which had been penned into its final form by Timothy Matlack, a calligrapher.

Even though it had been more than a year since the first shots fired at Lexington and Concord, the Declaration of Independence seemed to breathe new, determined breath into the war efforts. There was a long fight ahead of them, but they felt a certainty that they would win their freedom.

General Washington moved his troops south to try to defend New York, which was met with disaster because of the sea access, rivers, and islands. Throughout the month of July, seven hundred British ships brought an army of tens of thousands from Nova Scotia. There was no way for Washington to defend New

> **F.Y.I.** During the Revolution, there were at least fifty thousand "Tories" or Loyalists, who fought with the British against their fellow Americans.

Chapter 7

York against the British General Howe. The Americans narrowly escaped by using a motley fleet of various old fishing boats, rowboats, and sailing boats to cross to temporary safety on Manhattan Island.

After General Howe had taken New York, Washington and his men retreated to Trenton, New Jersey. Howe sent his Hessian soldiers to keep tabs on Washington and his men. The American army's morale was low. They had not won a battle in seven months, and Washington was facing the impending expiration of his men's enlistments at the end of December. General Washington knew if his men went home, he would be left with only fourteen hundred men. He desperately needed to do something to build morale, keep his men, and entice new recruits; he needed a victory!

Washington rose to the occasion and employed a brave and risky plan. He and his men crossed the Delaware River late on Christmas night. Silently, they rowed between the chunks of floating ice under the cover of the dark. The next morning, the Americans surprised the Hessians, capturing over nine hundred of them. The British response was quick, but Washington knew they would be hot on his heels. Leaving decoy campfires burning, the American army slipped out of camp, made their way around the British general, Cornwallis, and marched north to Princeton. The brave actions of General Washington brought hope to the Americans. The British knew the victories had stoked the freedom fire in the Americans' hearts again.

The British started to understand that these Americans were going to be a little harder to beat than they originally had thought. Their plan was to create a threesome of offensive action. Three generals, General Howe, General John Burgoyne, and General Barry St. Leger, would form a network of attacks, eventually coming together at Albany, New York. If this plan had worked, the British would have successfully cut off New England and upper New York, both centers of colonial resistance, from the rest of the colonies. As it was, the British generals made disastrous mistakes. Their timing and execution of their grand plan was clumsy, and their overall success was thwarted.

Chapter 7

> **General Washington was well-known to be a praying man. There are many accounts of how the general would spend quiet time with God, asking for guidance, and praying for his men and the future of their country. What are your thoughts about this? Do you think General Washington's prayers had anything to do with the startling clumsiness the three, great, British generals displayed? Do you think it was God confusing their path and plan?**
>
> *What do you think?*

The ensuing Battle of Saratoga ended in American victory and knocked one of the British armies out of the war. It also forced Britain to give up hope of ever conquering the northern colonies. Besides giving new hope to the Americans, the Battle of Saratoga also brought the French into the war on the American side. Even though the Americans had experienced a great victory at Saratoga, the American army was in rough shape. The French were still trying to decide how much help to give to the Americans, and winter was settling in again. General Washington's men were going to face the hardest time yet.

Section 2:

Washington and his men spent the winter of 1777-1778 at Valley Forge, Pennsylvania. Food, clothing, and shelter were in short supply. The weather was bitter, and sickness was abundant. The men's morale sank along with the temperatures. It was during this bitter winter that God sent help in the form of a Prussian officer, Baron Von Steuben (STOO-ben). Many of the men who constituted the American army were still largely untrained in military technique; Von Steuben took it upon himself to remedy this. Any man strong enough to handle the strenuous exercise was trained in hand to hand combat, weapon handling, and other helpful techniques.

By spring, morale had returned along with warmer temperatures. Supplies were still not abundant, however. The slim pocketbook of the Continental Army contained only monies from donations given by some of the wealthier colonials. The paper money system had collapsed, leaving the budget as slim pickings, indeed! Robert Morris, the head of the Department of Finance, arranged a loan of four million dollars from France and proceeded to stretch the money in many frugal directions.

Chapter 7

As General Washington and Baron Von Steuben worked diligently to help the army in the east, a British colonel named Henry Hamilton was causing quite an issue in the Ohio River Valley. Unfortunately, the colonel was paying the Native American Indians a rather large bounty for American scalps. The "Hair Bounty" led to the massacre of many western settlers. An American officer, George Roger Clark, gathered a force of one hundred seventy-five men to drive the under-handed Hamilton out of the area. Bravely, Clark and his men worked through the dense, dark forests, swamps, and rivers to capture two of the frontier outposts, so crucial to their success. (The capture of these two small frontier forts, Kaskaskia, in Illinois, and Vincennes, in Indiana, allowed the United States to later claim and settle lands along the Mississippi River.)

While the brave American army was facing unimaginable hardship in the battles on land, the equally brave navy was facing the almost-impossible task of fighting the British navy, which was well known to be the strongest in the world. The American navy was tiny, insignificant really. The odds were so stacked against them, in fact, that only someone bent on destruction would even volunteer! After France came into the war, the odds tipped a little more in America's favor, but it was still not an easy fight.

John Paul Jones

The most famous of all Revolutionary War naval officers was John Paul Jones. A Scotsman by birth, Jones had a fiery temper, a determination to win, and an almost insatiable appetite for adventure. One of the most famous sea battles of the Revolutionary War was because of Jones' stubborn determination.

John Paul Jones sailed his rotten tub of a ship (a refurbished French ship, the *Bonhomme Richard*, named after Benjamin Franklin's *Poor Richard's Almanac*) alongside of a British warship, the *Serapis*. As the mighty British frigate tore holes up and down the side of the *Bonhomme Richard*, Jones ordered his crew to lash the two ships together. The British commander yelled above the roar of the cannon, "Do you surrender?" to which Jones famously replied, "I have not yet begun to fight!" As the *Bonhomme Richard* filled with water,

Chapter 7

Jones and his men cleared the deck of the British frigate by throwing a hand grenade into an open hatch. While the British sailors were scrambling for cover, the Americans boarded the *Serapis*, took control of the ship, and unlashed the *Bonhomme Richard*. The damaged ship sank to the bottom of the ocean, her American flag still hoisted.

After the American win at Saratoga, the British turned their attention toward the south. Savannah and Augusta, Georgia, fell to the British forces as did Charleston, South Carolina. American forces failed to stop the British on any front, and the future began to look bleak for their cause of independence. General Nathanael Greene managed to harass the enemy forces enough to keep them from regrouping into a solid front, but the outcome was not a solid victory.

In the fall of 1780, the British colonel Patrick Ferguson proclaimed to all frontiersmen of the Carolina Piedmont region that they should come and lay down their weapons. If they chose to ignore his demands, he promised to "lay waste to the countryside with fire and sword." His words struck a fury in the hearts of the Americans. Their answer was simple. The men crossed the mountains in search of this impudent British officer. This militia group, called the "Over-mountain Men," met the challenge by capturing or killing the entire force of a thousand men.

Following this decisive victory, General Greene and Daniel Morgan won a strong victory at Cowpens, South Carolina, on January 17, 1781. Two months later, on March 15, Greene challenged Cornwallis near Greensboro, North Carolina. Even though Cornwallis won that battle, he did so at an extremely high price. The cost to win that battle eventually contributed to his ultimate downfall. Greene retreated, and Cornwallis chased him. The British supply line stretched out like the tail of a kite, weaving its way through the wilderness. As the supply line tried to keep up with the British army, American guerilla fighters attacked and harassed them at every turn.

When Cornwallis pulled out of the Carolina midlands, he led his troops toward Virginia, where he believed he would be safer. Little did Cornwallis know, but he was walking straight into a trap. The French had sent twenty-eight ships up from the West Indies under the command of General de Grasse, and General Washington was coming down from the north.

Chapter 7

Cornwallis was not prepared and became trapped at Yorktown. There was no way out; Cornwallis was forced to surrender. America had won!

Even though the war was officially over, Britain still had troops stationed throughout the colonies. There was conflict between the Loyalists and Patriots for quite some time. The Loyalists and British troops did not want to give up control over the forts in the frontier. Peace treaties were negotiated in Paris, because France had been the main American ally during the war. Benjamin Franklin, John Jay, and Henry Laurens were sent as the American negotiators. Benjamin Franklin suffered from a kidney stone attack, and Laurens was captured and held in the Tower of London, leaving John Jay to be the main negotiator. Henry Laurens was freed just in time to sign the Treaty of Paris.

Chapter 8 — The Treaty of Paris and the Confederation of the Colonies

America was finally free and independent! During the War for Independence, the colonies had been governed by the First and Second Continental Congress. Even though the colonies were rather reluctant to submit to a central government, the war had proven the importance of such a governing body; it was becoming increasingly evident that a new type of government was desperately needed to replace the British rule. In 1776, a committee had been appointed to submit a new plan for a better system of government. The solution was a confederation, a relatively simple and loose league or association of states.

In 1777, a new plan, called the Articles of Confederation, was written and brought before the Continental Congress. John Dickinson, the main author of the document, was a representative from Delaware. The Articles of Confederation stated that the governing body, or Congress, would have members who were elected on a yearly basis.

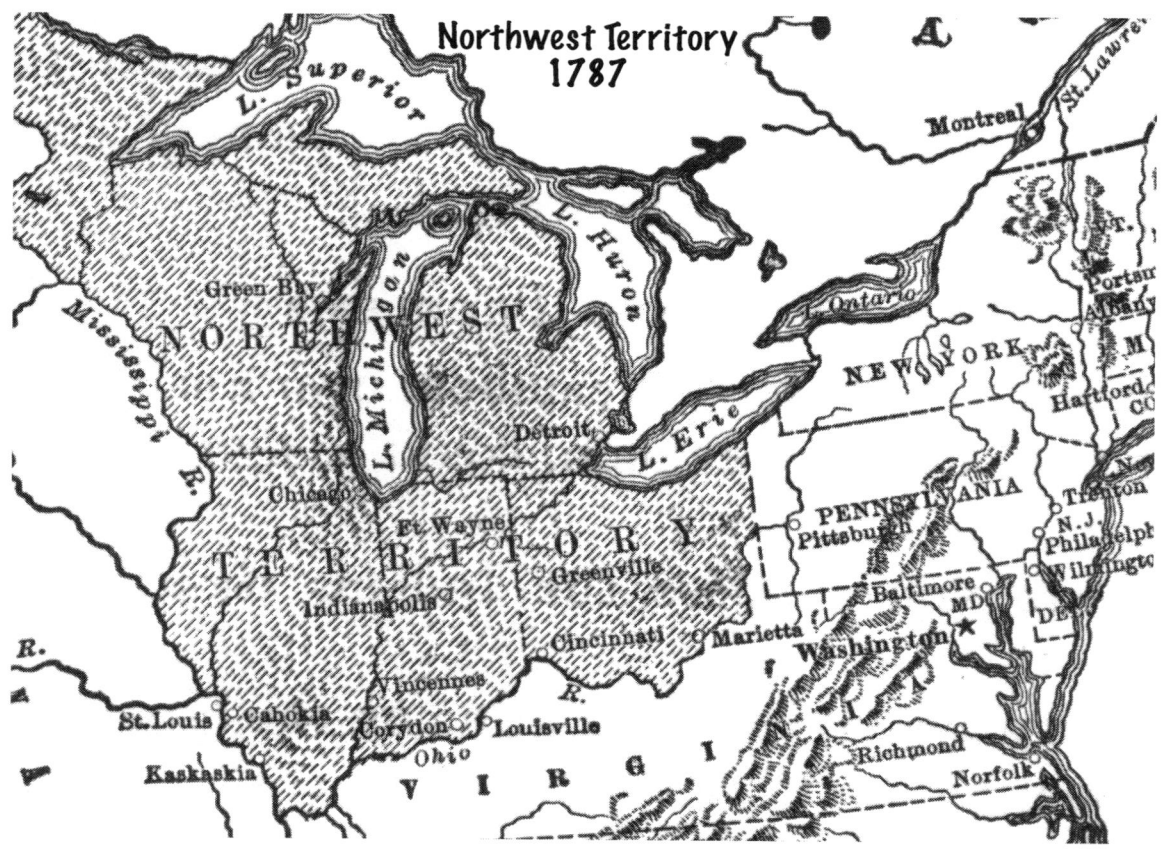

Chapter 8

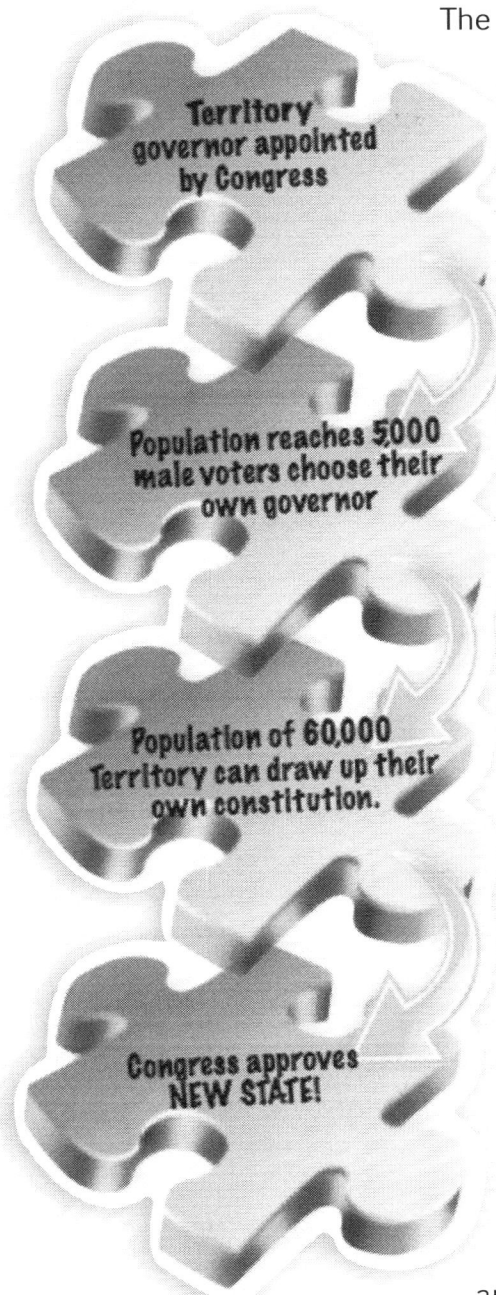

The states were not accustomed to having to work together in a timely fashion, and it took four years to complete the ratification process. The biggest hold-up was an argument about the western lands given in the Treaty of Paris. Representatives from the smaller, coastal states did not want the larger states, which bordered these new lands, to automatically receive more land. The argument was finally settled by two land ordinances. These ordinances governed how land was divided up into territories and what those territories had to do to become a state. Under the Northwest Ordinance of 1787, each one of these territories had a governor assigned by Congress. When a territory had five thousand adult, white males of voting age, they could elect their own governor. When the population of the territory reached sixty-thousand settlers, the people could write a constitution for their state and submit it to Congress. If their constitution guaranteed a republic form of government, they were accepted into the Union as a state. After they became a state, they had all of the same rights as all of the other original states. Interestingly, the Northwest Ordinance made the Ohio River the dividing line between slave states and territories and free, non-slave states. This ordinance was key to the healthy growth of the country in the future. It guaranteed equal rights to all states, old and new, big and small.

This new congress, the Confederation Congress, also set other crucial examples. For instance, it was the Confederation that started publishing its proceedings, which developed into today's Congressional Record. We can also thank the

> **F.Y.I.** It was Thomas Jefferson, the writer of the Declaration of Independence, who is mainly credited for drafting the Land Ordinances of 1785 and 1787.

63

Chapter 8

Confederation Congress for developing the first money system based on the decimal system of tens and hundreds. As you can see, although the Confederation lasted only eight years, it did accomplish some lasting good for our country.

The Confederation Congress had more power than the Continental Congress, but it did not have the power to tax. Even though the Confederation Congress could issue money, they did not have the power exclusively; if individual states wanted to issue their own money, there was no law against it. In other words, there was no federal currency. It took a lot of compromise to get the states to work together. They had to agree to accept each other's birth and death certificates, as well as marriage certificates.

Because of the wisdom behind the land ordinance legislation, the United States became one growing republic instead of new states being controlled by the original 13 colonies-turned-states. *What do you think?*

Although the Confederation Congress had accomplished a lot of good for our new country in its eight short years, it also failed in some crucial ways. To be fair to the Congress, the weakness actually was in the Articles of Confederation themselves, not in what the Congress did or didn't do. When it came down to it, the Articles of the Confederation did not specify the power to anyone in particular. The organizational weakness of the Articles was almost painful! They gave the Confederation Congress no true power to enforce the few laws they did outline. There were no separate branches of government to handle particular responsibilities.

As time passed, it became painfully evident that the Confederation Congress really didn't have any control over the economic atmosphere either. For example, the Congress had no right to levy taxes or enforce consequences for those refusing to pay the taxes that were in place. Because they didn't have the power to tax, they didn't have the power to gather necessary funds to run the government. Of course, this meant that debts went unpaid

Chapter 8

to soldiers, who had fought in the Revolution, and to the foreign aid loan from France. Everything was truly a mess.

The currency issue was also becoming disastrous. Many of the separate states were still using their own coins, which completely tangled up the money value that the Confederate Congress tried to set into place. In some locations in the states, creditors gained control of state legislatures and piled on illegal taxes to pay off state debt. When small farmers and their families could not pay these taxes, the court came in and confiscated their property. As the Confederation fell apart, the citizens of the new country, the United States, wondered if they were going to survive or if a foreign power would see their weakness and conquer them.

Poor foreign relations escalated. A general lack of respect for the new government fueled many disagreements. Britain still had some of their troops in the western forts they had controlled before the war, and British ships were stopping and harassing American ships. American ships were being bullied by pirates and forced to pay tribute. This was an insult, because it insinuated that the country was too weak to take care of itself.

England wasn't the only country causing trouble for our new nation. France was also quickly becoming impatient and annoyed. As the years passed and America was unable to repay the war loans, France became irritated. Spain was also an issue. Because Spain had substantial holdings of land in North America, the United States were nervous about the Spanish intentions. Americans watched anxiously as Spain convinced the Native American Indians to raid frontier settlements. Spain also refused to allow the Americans to use the lower Mississippi ports for trade.

The Confederation Congress had not gained an outstanding amount of respect on the home front either. By the summer of 1786, many farmers were being forced into bankruptcy because of the heavy taxes, and angry mobs of them were protesting. Daniel Shays, a veteran of the Continental Army, led the mob toward a federal arsenal. The situation was brought under control without any fatalities, but the disturbance did bring attention to the voice of the people.

Chapter 8

When George Washington heard about Shays' Rebellion, he was mortified. He believed that this type of civil rebellion made his young nation look "more contemptible" than ever. The Congress voted to call a convention with the express purpose of creating a government better able to cope with the necessary issues of the young country. The Philadelphia Convention would be a meeting to settle the question of what kind of government the United States of America would have. Everyone knew that the country could not continue with the Articles of Confederation the way they were.

For the People, by the People

Chapter 9: The Constitutional Convention

Chapter 10: The Founders and Framers - Part 1

Chapter 11: The Founders and Framers - Part 2

Chapter 12: The Great Debate: Federalists versus Anti-Federalist

Please leave blank.

Chapter 9 — The Constitutional Convention

Before we learn about the Constitutional Convention, let's talk about a few of the different types of government. The Founders were knowledgeable about the kind of government that had been tried, with some success, in ancient Athens and a few of the other Greek city-states. These city-states were directly run by the citizens, who met together in large groups to discuss and solve problems that affected them all; this is called a **direct democracy**. This type of government only worked until the population grew too large to support such discussions. As populations grew, the government needed to step up and do more. The problem was that the government had too many options from which to choose, and not enough power to make a decision. Because no one was truly in charge, the city-states became more and more unruly. Eventually, they resorted to mob rule and to dictatorship. What you need to remember is, a direct democracy is a government where each person has a direct say in their government.

The Founders knew that a direct democracy would not work for the United States. However, they did want the government to be for the people, by the people. They decided that a **representative democracy** was what we needed. The ancient Greek philosopher, Plato, called this type of government a **Republic**. In a representative democracy, the people still have a voice and the responsibility to use that voice, but they do so through a system of representatives. These representatives are elected and hold offices established for the people, by the people. In this way, there is a balance of power and a more organized approach to solving issues and dealing with injustice.

* * * * * * * * * * * * * * * *

The Philadelphia convention was one of the most important events in our history to date. God knew who needed to be there, and the men, who gathered there, were some of the most intelligent, talented men in American history. This convention was truly unprecedented in history; never before had this kind of government been designed. Never before had men come together to make a government for the people, by the people.

Chapter 9

It had been decided that the Philadelphia Convention would meet on May 14, 1787, but on the appointed day, only a dozen men arrived. It was eleven uneasy days later, on May 25th, that enough of the delegates had arrived, and the Convention could finally convene. Eventually, fifty-five men attended the Philadelphia Convention, held in Independence Hall. Wisely, the delegates met in secret to discuss their ideas for the new government. The summer of 1787 was one of the warmest in Philadelphia's memory, and the closed windows and doors did nothing to add comfort to the stuffy hall.

George Washington was elected as the president of the convention; his quiet strength was somehow reassuring. Some have said that it was Washington's presence at the Philadelphia Convention that made it a success, because he provided crucial balance and control. Respect for this man ran deep throughout the country; his position as a leader was not questioned by anyone.

Also at the Philadelphia Convention was a man who is often called the "Father of the Constitution." James Madison was a small man in stature, but he made up for it with his knowledge of law, government, and the workings of his country. Benjamin Franklin was the oldest delegate present at the convention. At the age of eighty-two, Franklin had been involved with every important event in the making of our country. Out of the group of men we call our Founding Fathers, Franklin is the only one who signed the Declaration of Independence in 1776, the Treaty of Alliance, Amity, and Commerce with France in 1778, the Treaty of Peace between England, France, and the United States (the Treaty of Paris) in 1782, and the Constitution in 1787. New York's leading delegate at the convention, Alexander Hamilton, favored a strong central government - one that "could stand like a Hercules."

Some of the leading men of the Revolutionary time period were absent. Thomas Jefferson was serving as minister to France, while the stalwart John Adams was minister to Great Britain. Samuel Adams, John Hancock, and Patrick Henry had not been selected to represent their states at the convention either. The baton had been passed to a new set of soldiers in the cause for freedom for our country.

Chapter 9

As the delegates began discussing the shortfalls of the Articles of Confederation, it became more and more clear that they needed to go back to the drawing board. The need to craft an all new government was a daunting one. How could they start from scratch and design a long lasting constitution, outlining the control and responsibilities of the new government? When you consider the fact that states were not used to working together on anything, the results of the convention are nothing short of a miracle.

As the delegates rolled up their sleeves and set to work, they discovered there were several fundamental issues they could agree upon. One of the most important of these issues was the need for a stronger central government. They had learned from experience that a weak central government, which gave no one in particular any control, was not an option. The new central government needed to have the power to affectively handle any potential problems that would eventually arise. There needed to be a division of powers, to supply a check and balance within the government. The delegates agreed that there should never be a situation where one person could take all of the control over the country.

The delegates also agreed on a second extremely important issue. They decided that the new government needed to be a representative republic. So, why did they choose a republic instead of a democracy? The leaders of our nation had learned several hard lessons through the period of taxation and rule of Britain, the Revolutionary period, and the hard years of the Articles of the Confederation. They had learned that the voice of the minority is often out-shouted when there are large masses deciding the rule. This is why they specified in the Constitution what each branch of government was for and what their responsibilities were to the people. They made it abundantly clear what the branches could and could not do.

In a democracy, the rules for governing could be changed whenever the wishes of the majority changed. They wanted to create a government that could not change unless the people voted on a change to the Constitution. Little did the delegates know, but the government that they were Providentially guided to devise would become the model of many governments that followed.

Chapter 9

The men, gathered in Independence Hall, were familiar with *Spirit of the Laws*, a book written by a French philosopher, Montesquieu (MON-tuh-SKYOO). In this book, Montesquieu outlined the three branches of government - executive, legislative, and judicial. As Montesquieu suggested in his book, the delegates at the convention desired a balance of power. It wouldn't help to have a government designed with three branches if each one did not have an express purpose; they needed to be interdependent.

The delegates wanted Americans as individuals to have rights and privileges. These men knew that they would have to compromise to reach the balance they needed. By the time the Constitution was a finished product, it was a whole bundle of compromises! Even so, the Constitution was deemed "the most wonderful work ever struck off at a given time by the brain and purpose of man" (William Gladstone, a prime minister of Britain in the nineteenth century). So what were some of the compromises? During the Philadelphia Convention, the disagreements involved two groups. The first disagreement was centered around how each state would have votes in Congress. The second disagreement concerned the issue of slavery.

James Madison's Virginia Plan, also sometimes called the Large State Plan, stated that the new government would have two legislative houses made up of representatives based on a state's population. This plan did not bode well with the smaller states. New Jersey representative, William Paterson, proposed another plan called the New Jersey Plan, or the Small State Plan. This plan advocated one legislative house composed of the same number of representatives from each state.

During the ensuing debate, Roger Sherman of Connecticut proposed the Great Compromise. This compromise provided for two legislative assemblies. In the house called the Senate, each state would be equally represented. Two senators from each state would serve in the Senate. In the House of Representatives, the representatives would be based on population. This compromise would preserve the power of the smaller states, while allowing the larger states to represent all of their people. The population of the states would be decided every ten years by a federal census.

Chapter 9

The argument about how the south could count the slaves there was also settled through a compromise. Since taxes were levied according to a state's population, should they count the slaves as people? If they were counted as people, equal with the whites, then they also should be given the other privileges and freedoms given to peoples of the population. The argument about how the slaves should be counted was settled through the Three-Fifths Compromise. A slave would be counted as three-fifths of a free person in the figuring of both taxes and representatives in that state. It makes me sad to have to tell you that this compromise also included a clause which promised that for twenty years, Congress would make no laws interfering with slavery.

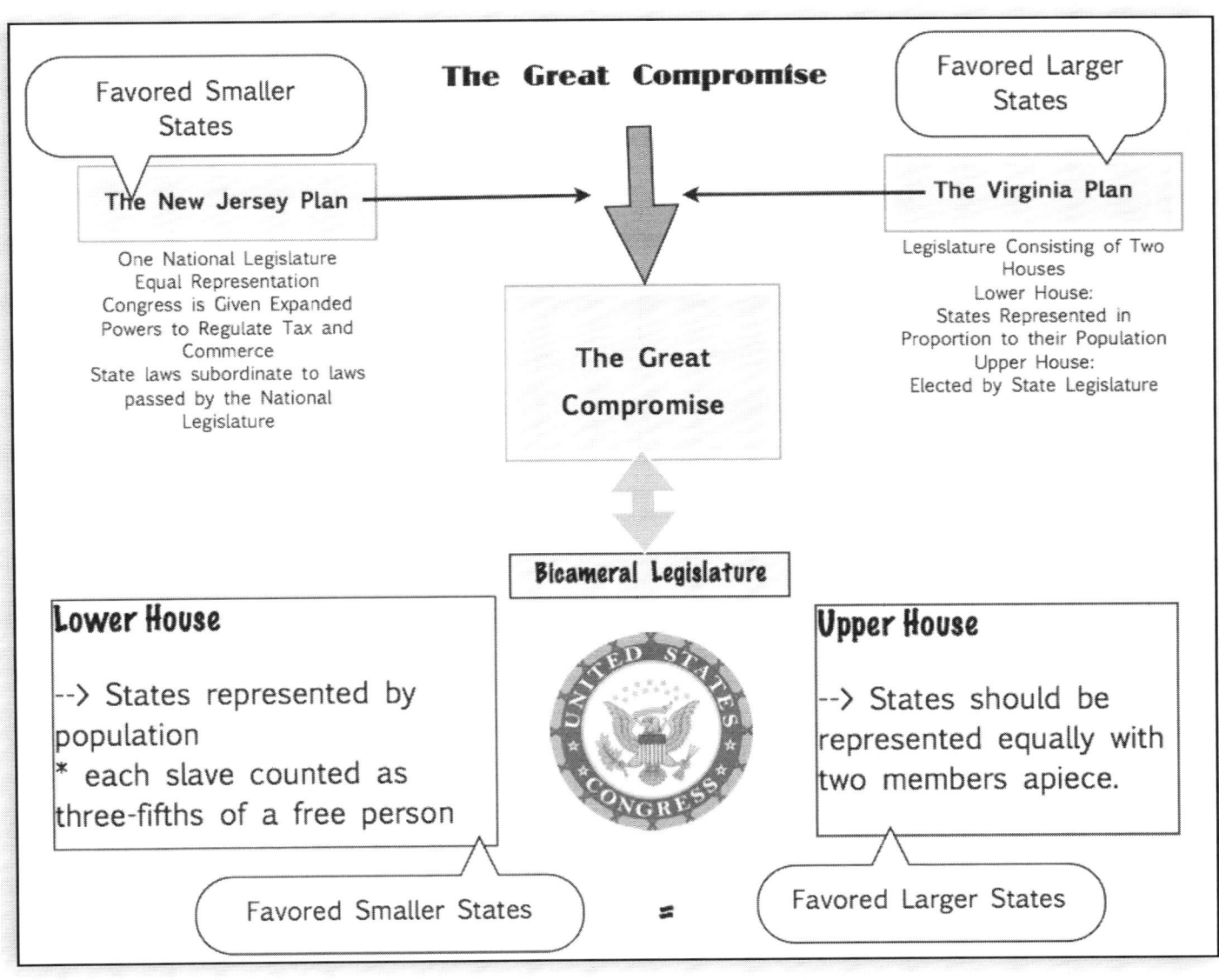

Chapter 9

The final compromise was the Commerce Compromise. The northern states wanted Congress to pass laws protecting them from foreign competition. They disagreed with the southern states over Congress' rights to pass navigation and tariff laws. The southern states were worried that these types of laws would lead to higher prices on goods that they needed to buy. The Commerce Compromise favored the North by allowing the laws to be passed by a simple majority instead of a two-thirds vote like the South requested.

Chapter 10 — Founders and Framers Part 1

In the next two chapters of this study, we will become acquainted with a number of the most important men in our country's past. Some of these men were what we call "Founders" or "Founding Fathers." These are the men who laid the foundations for the country to be successfully built by those who came after them. As we look closely at the lives of these courageous men in these chapters, you will see that they came from various walks of life, differing ethnic backgrounds, and a myriad of religious preferences. As you read some of their words in our next chapter, you will also observe the one factor they all have in common - the love of freedom and the belief that they could make a country unlike any other nation before them.

Doctor Benjamin Rush

The first hero of American history that we will study is a man who, throughout history, is called the "Father of American Medicine." Dr. Benjamin Rush is one of my favorite heroes of our country and of our faith. A man of great faith, great dedication, and great love for our country, Dr. Rush gave many years of his life to help the birth of our new nation.

Dr. Benjamin Rush was an innovator, a medical doctor, a signer of the Declaration of Independence, and a close friend to Thomas Jefferson and John Adams. He graduated from Princeton University at the age of fourteen and went on to study medicine in England and France. When Dr. Rush wrote essays in favor of American independence, people wondered why a medical doctor would be involved in politics, but he was the type of man who was not only interested in the body of a person, but in the whole of their being.

In 1776, he was sent as a delegate from Philadelphia to the Continental Congress to sign the Declaration of Independence, and during the Revolutionary War, Dr. Rush was enlisted as one of the chief physicians. After the war, Dr. Rush is known for staying out of the "ugliness" between the political parties. His love for Christ,

75

Chapter 10

his steadfastness, and his patriotism were the foundation of his character, and because of this, he was made president of the U.S. Mint by three presidents, all from various political parties. When asked to which political party he aligned himself, Benjamin Rush answered, "I am a 'Christocrat'... not a aristocrat or a Democrat."

Because of his staunch belief in freedom, equality, and the love of Christ for all mankind, Dr. Rush was an extremely outspoken advocate of the abolition movement. He worked tirelessly with Richard Allen, who founded the African Methodist Episcopal Church, and partnered with Benjamin Franklin to start the first anti-slavery movement. He was also involved in helping found the Sunday school movement and Bible society - an organization that helped produce the first mass-produced American Bible. Dr. Rush believed firmly that every home in America should have access to a Bible printed in America, for Americans.

As a medical doctor, Dr. Rush experimented extensively with medicine. He often used his own digestive system to explore gastric acid by using various and sundry combinations of food. Dr. Rush is credited for finding a cure for lockjaw (now called tetanus), a terrible bacterial disease that affects the nervous system.

Benjamin Rush worked at Pennsylvania Hospital for thirty years. During the horrible, deadly, and mysterious plague of yellow fever in 1793, over a tenth of the city's population died in one hundred days. Doctors all over the city were closing down their offices and fleeing for their lives, but Dr. Rush refused to go. Instead, he worked to find a cure and to give his patients hope. He is credited for saving thousands of people's lives.

"I may fall victim to the epidemic, and so may you gentlemen, but I prefer, since I have been placed here by divine Providence, to fall in performing my duty." Dr. Benjamin Rush. (1)

Dr. Benjamin Rush, hero of the Revolution, believer in equality, and Father of American Medicine died on April 19, 1813. He is buried in Christ Church Burial Grounds in Philadelphia, Pennsylvania.

Chapter 10

Haym Salomon (also spelled Solomon)

Our next hero of early American history is an extremely interesting man. Haym Salomon was not the conventional colonial American. In fact, Haym wasn't originally from America. Born in Poland, Haym was a Jewish broker, who immigrated to New York during the American Revolution. He would become the first financier to help keep America afloat during the Revolutionary War.

Haym's expertise was not limited to finances, however. He also served as a spy and was caught and imprisoned by the British. When they found out that he could speak fluent German, they made him an interpreter for the Hessians (hired German soldiers). He interpreted the orders but also added his own bits of information about the opportunities in America. Eventually, Haym was released and returned to America, where he married Rachel Heilbron. The couple would eventually have a home full of children.

Haym was instrumental in helping wounded soldiers, which eventually led to his capture a second time. The British scheduled his execution for August 11, 1778, but his Patriot friends would not hear of letting this happen; they smuggled him a message with an escape route, which he followed to freedom.

In 1781, Haym began to work extensively with the newly appointed Superintendent for Finance, Robert Morris. When George Washington knew his war chest was empty, and there was no place to turn for the monies needed for his campaign at Yorktown, Morris told him that there were no funds and no available credit. General Washington simply said, "Send for Haym Salomon." It was Haym who helped supply Washington's troops during the closing days of the war and raised money to get the French troops to the United States to fight the important battle at Yorktown. Through the sale of bills of exchange, Salomon raised twenty thousand dollars for Washington and his troops.

In 1782, Morris and Salomon knew that we needed a national bank. Haym Salomon and his Jewish friends bought shares in the first subscription of the National Bank of North

Chapter 10

America. These families, led by the example of Haym Salomon, are true heroes of American history. They completely supported the Patriot cause and gave everything they had to the cause of freedom. Haym Salomon died unexpectedly at the age of forty-five, on January 6, 1785. He is buried in the Mikveh Israel Cemetery in Philadelphia.

Noah Webster

When you hear the name "Webster" you probably think of a dictionary, and you would be right! We can thank Noah Webster for the way we spell, pronounce, and write many words in our American English language. Noah Webster wasn't simply a etymologist and lexicographer; he was a Bible translator, a soldier, a writer, an educator, a judge, as well as a public servant who served in the legislature.

Noah Webster was born into a family of great distinction. His father, Noah Sr., was descended from John Webster, a Connecticut Governor of great renown. Noah's mother, Mercy, was a descendant of Governor William Bradford, leader of the Pilgrims and governor of Plymouth Colony for about thirty years. Noah was schooled at home by his mother, who spent long hours teaching her children spelling, mathematics and music. His early education at home (until the age of six!) must have spoiled Noah educationally, for when he went to a one room primary school, he described his teachers as the "dregs of humanity." This experience inspired Noah to improve the American school system later in life.

By the age of fourteen, Noah was learning Latin and Greek from his church pastor, in preparation for his entrance to Yale College. Noah was an outstandingly intelligent young man! At the age of (almost) sixteen, he went to Yale. While he was there, he left to fight with the Connecticut Militia in the Revolutionary War. After four years at Yale, Noah set out on his own. Unfortunately, he did not have a clear plan of what he wanted to do with his life. Noah was mostly interested in law, but he needed a job to sustain himself. Through the years, he worked and studied, eventually passing his bar exam.

Chapter 10

Noah also wrote articles and gave speeches about what he wanted for America. He became known as an outspoken and learned proponent of a free America, independent from England or any other power. After the war was won and it became painfully apparent that the Articles of Confederation needed a major overhaul, it was Noah, who first called for a Constitutional Convention. After the Constitution was finished, the delegates asked Webster to draft an essay in favor of the new government. Noah consented and dedicated the work to Benjamin Franklin.

Noah contemplated his experience in the school of his childhood. Over the years, he had thought about what he believed education should be grounded upon. In 1782, he started writing textbooks for the American schools. Noah wanted to make the English language more accessible to the people of America. In 1806, he began the work it would take to produce a dictionary for the American people. Noah studied approximately twenty languages in order to translate and define words from their lexical roots into English. His dictionary was published in 1828, and it introduced the American spelling of words. Noah's work standardized the way Americans spoke, helping to bring unity and continuity to our new nation. Noah Webster also authored *The Blue Back Speller*, which was not only a spelling book, but also taught morals and religious truths that helped unify the country and laid the foundation for American education.

> Inside the Blue Back Speller is this inscription in Noah Webster's honor: "The man who taught millions to read and none to sin." *F.Y.I.*

Chapter 11

Founders and Framers Part 2
Quotes of Our Fathers

Have you ever wondered what kind of people our Founding Fathers really were? Let's take time to read through some of their words spoken about the beginning of our country and government. The principles of our new government had already been woven into the fabric of the colonies, starting with the Pilgrims and their Mayflower Compact. The men who were instrumental in founding our country were a product of this type of culture.

"The general principles on which the fathers achieved independence were the general principles of Christianity that are as eternal and immutable as the existence and attributes of God." (a)

"Without religion, this world would be something not fit to be mentioned in polite company: I mean hell." (b)

"I always consider the settlement of America with reverence and wonder, as the opening of a grand scene and design in providence, for the illumination of the ignorant and the emancipation of the slavish part of mankind all over the earth." (c)

John Adams was a signer of The Declaration of Independence, a judge, a diplomat, one of two signers of the Bill of Rights, and the second President of the United States. He was also the father of John Quincy Adams, the sixth President of the United States of America. John and his wife, Abigail, were two heroes of the Revolutionary period.

Chapter 11

"The right to freedom being the gift of God Almighty, it is not in the power of man to alienate this gift and voluntarily become a slave... These may be best understood by reading and carefully studying the institutes of the great Law Giver and Head of the Christian Church, which are to be found clearly written and promulgated in the New Testament."

"We have this day restored the Sovereign to Whom all men ought to be obedient. He reigns in heaven and from the rising to the setting of the sun, let His kingdom come."

"Religion in a Family is at once its brightest Ornament and its best Security." (d)

Samuel Adams was a signer of the Declaration of Independence. He was called the "Father of the American Revolution"; he served as the governor of Massachusetts, and he was ratifier of the U.S. Constitution.

To the people of New Hampshire:
"...confess before God [your] aggravated transgressions and implore His pardon and forgiveness through the merits and mediation of Jesus Christ. . .that the knowledge of the Gospel of Jesus Christ may be made known to all nations, pure and undefiled religion universally prevail, and the earth be filled with the glory of the Lord." (e)
Proclamation of a day of fasting and Prayer

Josiah Bartlett was a military officer, signer of the Declaration of Independence, a judge, and the governor of New Hampshire.

Chapter 11

"The sacred rights of mankind are not to be rummaged for among old parchments or musty records. They are written, as with a sunbeam, in the whole volume of human nature, by the Hand of Divinity itself, and can never be erased or obscured by mortal power." (f)

"The fundamental source of all your errors, sophisms and false reasonings is a total ignorance of the natural rights of mankind. Were you once to become acquainted with these, you could never entertain a thought, that all men are not, by nature, entitled to a parity of privileges. You would be convinced, that natural liberty is a gift of the beneficent Creator to the whole human race, and that civil liberty is founded in that; and cannot be wrested from any people, without the most manifest violation of justice." (g)

Alexander Hamilton was a Revolutionary General, a signer of the Constitution, an author of the Federalist Papers, and Secretary of the Treasury.

"It is every American's right and obligation to read and interpret the Constitution for himself." (h)

"The practice of morality being necessary for the well being of society, He has taken care to impress its precepts so indelibly on our hearts that they shall not be effaced by the subtleties of our brain. We all agree in the obligation of the moral principles of Jesus and nowhere will they be found delivered in greater purity than in His discourses." (i)

"I predict future happiness for Americans, if they can prevent the government from wasting the labors of the people under the pretense of taking care of them." (j)

Thomas Jefferson was a signer of the Declaration of Independence, a diplomat, the governor of Virginia, Secretary of State, and the Third President of the United States.

Chapter 11

"The civil rights of none shall be abridged on account of religious belief or worship, nor shall any national religion be established." (k)

"A watchful eye must be kept on ourselves lest while we are building ideal monuments of Renown and Bliss here we neglect to have our names enrolled in the Annals of Heaven." (l)

James Madison is known as the "Father of the Bill of Rights." He was an author of the Federalists Papers, a representative from Virginia, the Secretary of State, and the fourth President of the United States.

"[I]t would be peculiarly improper to omit in this first official act my fervent supplications to that Almighty Being Who rules over the universe, Who presides in the councils of nations, and Whose providential aids can supply every human defect – that His benediction may consecrate to the liberties and happiness of the people of the United States a government instituted by themselves for these essential purposes." (m)

George Washington is often called the Father of Our Country. He was also a judge, a member of the Continental Congress, Commander-in-Chief of the Continental Army, the president of the Constitutional Convention, and the first true President of the Unites States.

Chapter 12
The Great Debate: Federalists versus Anti-Federalists

Since its ratification, the Constitution of the United States has been the steadfast guideline of our country's government. Those following the Constitution through the decades have labored to promote freedom. We must never take this for granted; a study of world history will quickly show you that governments have risen and fallen, leaving in their wake disaster for the their citizens. We must do everything in our range of responsibility to protect this guide, which was wrought through sweat, blood, and tears. We must protect our rights as Americans. I think for us to protect the Constitution, we need to know and understand how it became the rule of our land. After the Constitution was written, there were two separate parties, who battled out their differences in order to come to a compromise worthy of ratification.

The Anti-Federalist group was not as organized as the Federalists, but they had some prominent leaders in their midst including Patrick Henry. The men making up this group came from various locations around the country, and they came with varying opinions about what the government should look like. However, they were united by a core belief that the greatest threat to the country's future lay in the government's potential to become corrupt and seize power, therefore becoming a tyrannical rule. The aftertaste of British tyranny was still strong in their mouths, and they stood firmly against what they considered a potential disaster.

The Anti-Federalists wanted the bulk of the power to be in the individual states' hands, and they strongly believed that the government, with its President, Supreme Court, and two Houses of Legislature, was plainly too complicated. They were concerned that the voice of the people would become lost in the shuffle and noise of such a government. The Anti-Federalists believed that the citizens of the country - the common, middle class -

John Jay

Chapter 12

should help run the government.

Alexander Hamilton

The Federalists were in favor of a strong central government. They felt that they were the rightful heirs of the Revolution; after all, they claimed, it was their strong governmental leadership during the struggle for independence that had won the war and brought America through. The Federalist group had an impressive membership. Among their numbers were James Madison, Alexander Hamilton, and John Jay.

The Federalists argued that the Anti-Federalists' fears of a complicated government leading to tyranny were unfounded. They believed that by separating powers among the three branches - the executive to govern, legislative to make laws, and the judicial to enforce said laws - they could keep any one branch or person from taking control. The Federalists felt so strongly about the strength of the Constitution that they outlined their vision in *The Federalist*, known today as *The Federalist Papers*, a collection of essays by James Madison, Alexander Hamilton, and John Jay. These essays (which you will be studying in part) outline in great detail how our government is meant to work.

The Federalists eventually won most of the Great Debate, but only after the Anti-Federalists won a major victory - we can thank these men for the Bill of Rights. If it had not been for these brave men insisting on provisions in favor of the people, we would not have the first ten amendments to the Constitution. These rights include the basic freedoms that make America so appealing to so many people from all over the world. They include the freedom of speech, freedom of religion, freedom of the press and assembly, and the right to a trial by a jury of one's peers.

James Madison

These two groups, the Federalists and the Anti-Federalists, became the first two political parties of our country. The Federalists

Chapter 12

and their supporters believed in the Implied Powers Stance, which said there are powers, although not stated in the Constitution, that are implied by powers expressly stated. The Anti-Federalists took the Strict Power Stance, which stated that if the Constitution doesn't specifically grant the power, the government doesn't have the power.

**What do you think?
After studying what the Federalists and the Anti-Federalists stood for politically, with which group would you most align yourself?**

Over the next several weeks, you will be studying the three branches of the government and the Constitution, which outlines the responsibilities of each one. You will find that each of these branches has a distinct purpose. We will spend at least a week studying each one, ending with an overview and a look at our responsibilities in the upholding of our government.

The Legislative Branch makes laws.

The Executive Branch carries out laws.

The Judiciary Branch examines and interprets laws.

The Government of Our Country

Chapter 13: The Branches of Government, the Legislative Branch (1)

Chapter 14: The Branches of Government, the Legislative Branch (2)

Chapter 15: The Branches of Government, the Executive Branch

Chapter 16: The Branches of Government, the Judicial Branch

Chapter 17: More About Our Government and Constitution

Please Leave Blank.

Chapter 13

The Branches of Government
Part 1: The Legislative Branch

The lawmaking branch of our country's government is the legislature, which is known as Congress. Congress is a bicameral legislature; it has two bodies, the **House of Representatives** and the **Senate**. Each state has two representatives, called senators, in the Senate. The number of representatives in the House (of Representatives) depends on the population of each state. These members of the House are called congressmen. There are four hundred thirty-five members in the House of Representatives, while there are one hundred senators. As you are reading this, you have two senators and a varying number of representatives according to your state's population, representing you in the nation's capitol. Do you think they are representing you well?

Congress has much responsibility, because it is the branch that is meant to represent *We the People.* Besides having the power to make laws, Congress holds the purse strings of the nation, as well as serving as a check and balance for the other branches of government. No bill may become a law without the approval of both bodies of the Congress and the signature of the president. The exception to this is if the president does not attend to a bill for ten days after it has been presented to him. If this happens, the law will become a bill if the Congress approves of it and is still in session. (We will explore how laws are made in our next chapter, as well as discover which committees are in charge of certain responsibilities.)

Here is a list of duties performed by the Congress of our country. (1)

1. Makes laws
2. Coins money and fixes the value
3. Holds the right to decide the amount of federal taxes and to collect them
4. Has the power to borrow money for the United States government

89

Chapter 13

5. Controls trade and commerce between the United States and foreign powers
6. Establishes the armed forces and funds them
7. Works with the president to declare war
8. Establishes roads and post offices
9. Issues copyrights and patents
10. Regulates naturalization laws pertaining to immigration
11. Holds authority to admit new states into the Union
12. Can try and impeach the president
13. Must approve the president's appointments for certain jobs.

Although the duties of the Senate and the House are very similar, they are not identical. For example, the House has authority to impeach the president or charge him with misconduct. If this happens, the president stands trial by the Senate if he chooses not to resign from his office. It is also the Senate's job to confirm the president's appointments to the Supreme Court, cabinet members, ambassadors, and senior officers of the Armed Forces.

Requirements for congressmen and senators are slightly different also. A congressman must be at least twenty-five years old, as well as being a citizen of the United States for at least seven years and be a resident of the district he represents. Congressmen are elected every two years. A senator must be at least thirty years old and have been a United States citizen for nine years, as well as being a resident of of the state he represents. Senators are elected every six years.

This is what some of our founders said about writing this part of the Constitution.

James Madison

> The accumulation of all powers, legislative, executive and judiciary, in the same hands, whether of one, a few, or many, and whether hereditary, self-appointed, or elective, may justly be pronounced the very definition of tyranny.

Chapter 13

> For when you assemble a number of men to have the advantage of their joint wisdom, you inevitably assemble with those men, all their prejudices, their passions, their errors of opinion, their local interests, and their selfish views. From such an assembly can a perfect production be expected? It therefore astonishes me, Sir, to find this system approaching so near to perfection as it does.

Benjamin Franklin

James Madison

> It is ESSENTIAL to such a government that it be derived from the great body of the society, not from an inconsiderable proportion, or a favored class of it; otherwise a handful of tyrannical nobles, exercising their oppressions by a delegation of their powers, might aspire to the rank of republican, and claim for their government the honorable title of republic... The House of Representatives will derive its powers from the people of America;... The Senate, on the other hand, will derive its powers from the States, as political and coequal societies; and these will be represented on the principle of equality in the Senate, as they now are in the existing Congress.

> The role of vice president is the most insignificant office that ever the invention of man contrived or his imagination conceived.
> - In a letter to his wife Abigail

John Adams

Chapter 13

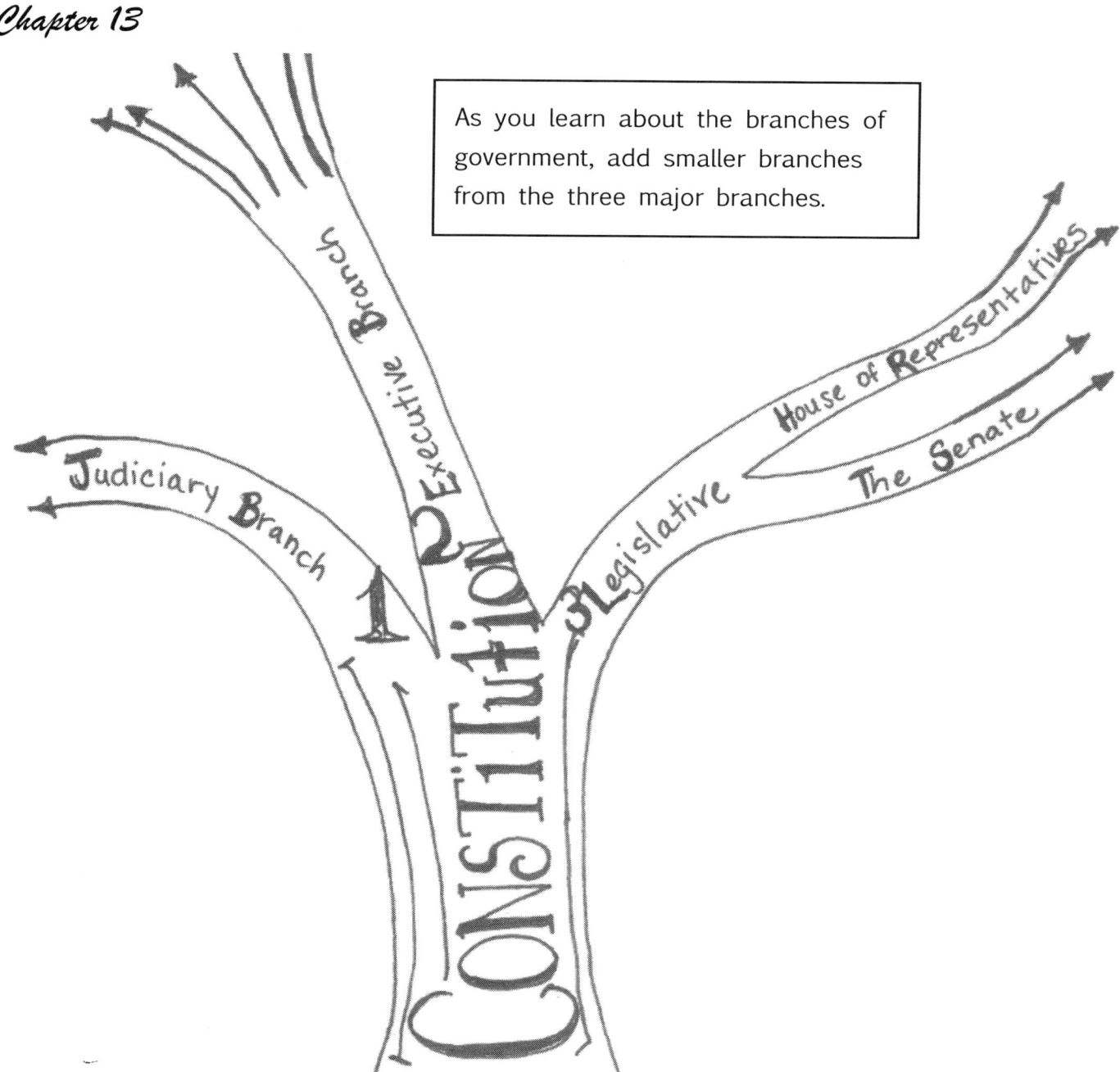

You will be creating a poster-size graphic of your own. Start this week by sketching a tree like the one in the graphic above. This week draw the Legislative Branch and label the Congress and Senate. You will be adding information to your graphic as you learn it.

Answers to the *Constitution Vocab Match*:

Bicameral Legislature-f.   Writ-c.   Impeachment-a.   gravitas-e.   Pro tempore-b.
Quorum-d.

Chapter 14 — The Branches of Government
The Legislative Branch
Part 1 Continued

In this chapter, we are going to examine how a law is made. This process can be somewhat confusing, so I urge you to take careful notes as you read through this chapter. It may be necessary to reread for retention. Your student journal contains pages to aid you in the study of the branches of government, as well as Constitutional study pages.

First, ideas for laws can come from various directions. They may come from a House or Senate member, or constituents - individual or corporate - can communicate proposals to their representatives through a petition. The Executive Branch can also propose legislation. The president, a cabinet member, or agency head can offer a draft of a proposed bill to the president of the Senate or to the Speaker of the House.

Proposals for a law are introduced to Congress in one of these four primary forms: the joint resolution, the simple resolution, the concurrent resolution, or the bill. The most common form used is the bill. A bill is always introduced by a member of the Congress, even though they may originate in the House of Representatives or the Senate, except when the bill concerns raising revenue. This type of bill always originates in the House of Representatives. When a bill originates in the House of Representatives, it is designated by the letters, "H.R." with a series of numbers following, while a bill originating in the Senate is designated by the letter, "S." followed by a series of numbers.

After a bill has been printed and introduced, it is sent to the appropriate committee. The responsible committee then studies, inspects, and very often, revises it. This scrutiny of the bill is the most important part of the process, because it is in this phase that potential dangers are discovered in the bills. The committees' responsibility is to make sure that the proposed law lines up with the needs of the citizens of our country.

Chapter 14

Congress uses these four types of committees: standing committees, joint committees, select (or special) committees, and conference committees. Both the House of Representatives and the Senate have standing committees. Most of these committees have subcommittees which address certain areas under their jurisdiction. When a bill is proposed and sent to a committee, the chairman of that committee sends it to the subcommittees for an initial inspection. This is the first round of scrutiny, which may end with a revision of the bill. The bill is then sent to the whole committee for inspection and scrutiny. If the bill is approved by the entire committee, it is then reported to the full House or Senate. If the committee refuses to take action on the bill, they can effectively kill it.

Here are the standing committees in the House of Representatives (in alphabetical order):

1. Agriculture
2. Appropriations
3. Armed Services
4. Budget
5. Education and Labor
6. Energy and Commerce
7. Financial Services
8. Foreign Affairs
9. Homeland Security
10. House Administration
11. Judiciary
12. Natural Resources
13. Oversight and Government Reform
14. Rules
15. Science and Technology
16. Small Business
17. Stands of Official Conduct
18. Transportation and Infrastructure
19. Veterans' Affairs
20. Ways and Means

Chapter 14

Here are the standing committees in the Senate (in alphabetical order):

1. Agriculture
2. Nutrition
3. Forestry
4. Appropriations
5. Armed Services
6. Banking
7. Housing
8. Urban Affairs
9. Budge
10. Commerce
11. Science
12. Transportation
13. Energy and Natural Resources
14. Environment and Public Works
15. Finance
16. Foreign Relations
17. Health
18. Education
19. Labor
20. Pensions
21. Homeland Security and Governmental Affairs
22. Judiciary
23. Rules and Administration
24. Small Business and Entrepreneurship
25. Veterans' Affairs

The House of Representatives organized the Rules Committee to help determine the order in which committee approved bills come to the floor. This committee has proved

Chapter 14

crucial because of the large number of representatives in the House. The Senate does not follow this protocol; leadership is responsible for scheduling the action.

Standing committees also oversee the operations of the executive departments under their jurisdiction by studying and providing facts to determine whether the departments are administering legislation the way it is intended. Other congressional studies are performed by select committees. These special committees are usually organized to study and to deal with specific subjects. A good example of this is the special committees from both the Senate and the House that are currently studying the problems that senior citizens are dealing with in the aging process. There are other select (or special) committees which study and address issues that children deal with, youth and family life, hunger across the nation, drug abuse and control, and intelligence.

Joint committees are committees shared by the House and the Senate, and they are used by Congress for study and administrative purposes. These committees are Economics, Printing, Library, and Taxation. Conference committees help work out the differences between similar and sometimes identical bills passed separately by the House and the Senate. These committees are not permanent; they are formed to work out the differences on a particular bill and then are dissolved afterward. All members of the House and Senate are required to work on these committees.

After the bill goes through all of the appropriate committees' scrutiny, it is finally brought to the floor for debate and possible amendments by the full House or Senate. The debate is followed by a vote whether to kill or pass the bill. If the bill does pass the vote, it is then taken to the other chambers, where it goes through the same committee and floor procedures. The bill has to eventually pass both the House and Senate in identical form before it can be sent to the president. The president can either sign the bill or veto it and send it back to Congress. If the president does veto the bill, Congress can override it by a two-thirds majority vote in both houses.

Chapter 15: The Branches of Government
Part 2: The Executive Branch

Our Constitution's Article 2 outlines the responsibilities of the Executive Branch of our government. The Executive Branch, which consists of the president, the vice-president, cabinet, departments, and numerous (independent) agencies to help carry the workload, enforces and carries out laws and policies.

The president serves a four year term with the possibility of reelection to a second term. A presidential candidate has to be a natural born citizen, at least thirty-five years old, and a resident of the the United States for a least fourteen years. The vice-president succeeds the president if the president is forced to vacate his office prematurely. As we learned earlier, the vice-president also resides over the Senate.

The United States president has a big load of responsibility. He is the Chief Executive of the federal government and the Commander-in-Chief of the entire United States armed forces. The president also appoints cabinet members, federal justices, military officers, ambassadors, ministers and consuls. The check of power comes from the mandatory two-thirds approval vote from the Senate. The president may also grant pardons and reprieves for federal crimes and draw up peace treaties with other nations - again, this must have a two-thirds approval Senate vote. We have learned that the president can veto a bill when it comes across his desk. This veto may be overridden by Congress with a two-thirds vote in Congress. You have probably heard of a special presidential address, called the State of the Union Address, on TV or on the radio. This special report, informing the citizens of the United States of the condition of our country, is the president's responsibility. Yet another responsibility is the president's authority to declare war. (Of course, he must ask Congress first.)

So, what is the cabinet? The main job of the cabinet is to consult and advise the president on important executive policy and administrative work. The cabinet consists of

Chapter 15:

fifteen department heads, which are known as secretaries. Here is a list of the departments and a synopsis of their responsibilities.

1. **Department of State** - handles foreign policy.

2. **Department of the Treasury** - financial agent and advisor to the president.

3. **Department of Defense** - advisor to the president on military matters.

4. **Department of Justice** - the attorney general appoints lawyers to handle federal criminal cases.

5. **Department of the Interior** - deals with three areas: Indian affairs, directs all U.S. territories, and serves as custodian of natural resources.

6. **Department of Agriculture** - forest service, oversees farming, soil conservation, and related areas.

7. **Department of Commerce** - deals with business and trading activities.

8. **Department of Labor** - promotes the welfare of all of the country's wage earners.

9. **Department of Health and Human Services** - oversees Welfare, the Food and Drug Administration, Medicare, and other health related areas.

10. **Department of Housing and Urban Development** - provides housing for the poor and promotes community development.

11. **Department of Transportation** - oversees the Coast Guard, the Federal Highway Administration and any other other area of transportation.

12. **Department of Energy** - develops alternative sources of energy.

13. **Department of Education** - has a goal to promote quality education to all Americans.

14. **Office of Homeland Security** - oversees efforts to defend Americans against domestic terrorism.

15. **Department of Veteran Affairs** - operates programs to benefit veterans and their families.

Chapter 15:

Before he can enter into the Execution of his Office, he shall take the following Oath or Affirmation: — "I do solemnly swear (or affirm) that I will faithfully execute the Office of President of the United States, and will to the best of my Ability, preserve, protect and defend the Constitution of the United States."

ARTICLE II, SECTION 1, CLAUSE 8

John Jay

[The Constitution] confines the electors to men of whom the people have had time to form a judgment, and with respect to whom they will not be liable to be deceived by those brilliant appearances of genius and patriotism, which, like transient meteors, sometimes mislead as well as dazzle.

John Adams

Liberty cannot be preserved without a general knowledge among the people.

Constitution Vocab Match answers:
Secede-b.   Oath of Office-d.   Unappropriated-a.   Czar-c.

Chapter 16 — The Branches of Government
Part 3: The Judicial Branch

In this chapter we will explore the final branch of our government, the Judicial Branch. Article 3 of our Constitution establishes the Judicial Branch, and because it is a shorter section to study in your Student Journal, we will spend more time studying the actual workings of the Judicial Branch in this chapter.

The Judicial Branch is responsible for interpreting the laws and establishing the procedures to apply them through the court system, and this can be a difficult process to understand. To put it simply, the Constitution charges the Judicial Branch to guard and to justly interpret our laws. In turn, this enables our country to be governed by constitutionally sound laws instead of by the whim of every powerful person in a high office of government. The original goal for this branch of government was peaceful settlement of disputes by administrating laws through a sound judicial process. We can thank our Founding Fathers for all of the checks and balances worked into our Constitution!

In medieval times, kings ruled with a heavy hand, and before the Magna Carta, these monarchs not only had the final say in everything that happened in their country, they could exempt themselves from the law if they wished. If someone had a dispute, they had to travel to the king's court, where advisors to the king would help him settle the argument. The people of the kingdom were lucky if they had a kind-hearted king, who wasn't given to bouts of moodiness, but if they happened to have a crabby monarch, their case might be settled in a less than honorable and fair way. In the United States, we do not have a king,* but we do have a court. Unlike in those of medieval times, in our courts, judges, lawyers, and juries come together to help their fellow citizens peacefully resolve legal disputes. We refer to this judicial process as a trial.

A trial is a legal examination and discussion about what each disputing party presents as their position. Each party brings evidence that supports their position before an impartial decision maker. In a trial, the person accused of the crime or wrongdoing is called the

Chapter 16

defendant. The plaintiff, the person or party bringing the accusation against the defendant, can be an individual or a designated government official (depending on the type of crime the defendant is being accused of). After the evidence is presented by both the defendant (and their lawyer) and the plaintiff, the judge or a jury (a group of citizens, who have no involvement in the dispute) decides the outcome of the dispute. We refer to the dispute, brought before the judge and jury, as a case. There are two types of cases in the judicial system:

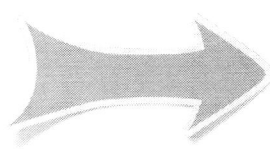

Criminal law cases -
These are cases involving a dispute in which the government is charging the defendant with committing a crime and breaking laws that protect other people's safety (i.e. - murder or burglary). A defendant convicted of one of these crimes would probably be sent to prison as punishment.

Civil law cases -
These are cases involving disputes among individual citizens or government officials, usually involving money or property. Unlike criminal cases, convicted defendants in civil cases usually pay money for a punishment instead of going to jail.

Take a moment to review some Judicial Jargon...

Review the definitions of each of these terms before moving on. You might find it helpful to make a list in your notebook or flashcards for review.

1. **Judicial** - anything related to laws and courts
2. **Judicial Branch** - the branch of our government which interprets the laws
3. **Court** - a place two parties may peacefully settle a dispute
4. **Plaintiff** - the accusatory party
5. **Evidence** - the facts that support a party's case in court
6. **Jury** - a group of citizens, who all must be uninvolved with the case
7. **Judicial process** - the process of examining evidence to settle a dispute
8. **Trial** - involves two parties coming together in a court of law to settle a dispute
9. **Defendant** - the party being accused of a crime or misconduct

Chapter 16

10. **Case** - a dispute that has been brought to a court to be settled
11. **Criminal law cases** - cases in which government officials are charging an individual with breaking a law, which protects another person's safety
12. **Civil law cases** - cases involving a dispute between two citizens, usually over money or property

Now let's take a look at the **anatomy of the Judicial Branch**. We have learned that the official purpose of the Judicial Branch is to interpret the constitutionality of laws. The Judicial Branch is made up of one Supreme Court, thirteen Courts of Appeals, and over ninety District Courts. Together these courts help keep the country's judicial system running as smoothly as possible.

Federal courts have jurisdiction of the following areas:

1. Disputes and civil actions between the states
2. Disputes and cases involving federal crimes
3. Lawsuits against foreign consuls and ambassadors
4. Cases against admiralty and maritime
5. Patent, copyright, and bankruptcy cases
6. Civil cases against the government - only in cases where consent to sue has been given
7. Civil suits between citizens of different states - only in cases involving above $10,000

The **Supreme Court** is at the **top of the Judicial Branch** of the government. It consists of nine justices (eight associate justices and the chief justice). The president appoints all of the justices after the Senate approves them. They have a life term as justice.

Chapter 16

-> If the Supreme Court decides a case, it is law of the land for all citizens of the country, but it can reverse a decision or nullify the law, declaring it to be unconstitutional.

-> The only types of cases originating in the Supreme Court: cases affecting ambassadors or other diplomatic personnel and cases in which states are parties.

-> All of the other cases arrive in the Supreme Court through the appellate route (through the Court of Appeals), through writ of certiorari.

    Writ = order issued in the name of the court

    Certiorari = call up for a review

    Writ of certiorari = an order by which a higher court calls upon a lower one to turn over the record in a given case for a review.

The **Court of Appeals** is immediately below the Supreme Court. There are thirteen Courts of Appeal.

-> 12 of the Courts of Appeal are geographically defined.

-> The 13th Court of Appeal is the United States Court of Appeals for the Federal Circuit. This Court of Appeals has nationwide jurisdiction over appeals based on their subject.

-> Each court has 4 - 26 permanent judges, who are appointed by the president and approved by the Senate.

-> The courts of appeals were established in 1891 to help keep the Supreme Court from having to handle all of the cases on appeal from the district courts. Now the Supreme Court reviews the decisions of the Courts of Appeal.

The **District Court** are the trial courts where the federal cases start out. From the district courts, appeals can move to the courts of appeal, or in some cases to the Supreme Court.

-> More than ninety district courts are located in the states.

Chapter 16

-> Districts have 1 to 27 judges who must reside in the district to which they were appointed.

-> Most cases begin at the district court level, and though some appeal cases are transferred to them, they do not start at this level.

-> Nearly all defendants accused of federal crimes are tried in district courts.

Besides these three types of courts, there are other courts that have been established by Congress to help meet specific needs that have come about over time. Some of these courts are the Tax Court, the Claims Court, and the Court of International Trade.

The State Court System...

Each state has its own court system to handle the cases involving their state laws. The court system at the state level is similar to that of the federal court system. Just like the federal level courts, states have state supreme courts, state courts of appeal, and state district courts.

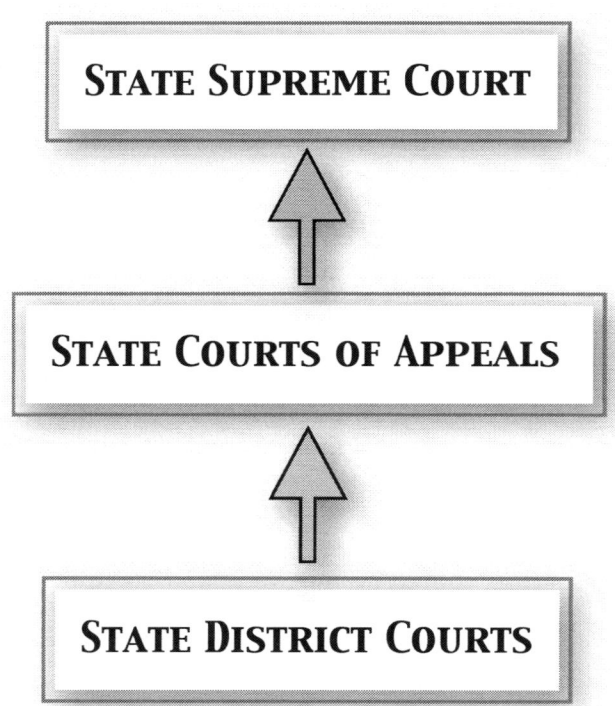

*Article 1, Section 9, Clause 8: "No Title of Nobility shall be granted by the United States: and no Person holding any Office of Profit or Trust under them, shall without the Consent of the Congress, accept of any present, Emolument, Office, or Title, or any kind whatever, from any King, Prince, or foreign State."

Chapter 17 — More About Our Government and Constitution

We are coming to the end of our study of the Constitution of our country. In this chapter, we will look at the last portion of the Constitution and what it establishes in our government. The Founding Fathers had worked hard to establish a government with plenty of checks and balances woven throughout its fabric. In the last four articles of the Constitution, they addressed other issues they could foresee their new nation encountering. They knew the states were not used to working with each other, and they knew this could cause some serious trouble. Thank goodness enough of the states agreed with the Constitution to ratify it! This truly was a miracle, considering how each state thought of themselves as sovereign in their own right.

By including the "Full Faith and Credit Clause," the Founding Fathers wrote into our constitution that the states were expected to treat each other as equals and respect each other's laws. This clause is extremely important in keeping our country united. It is this clause that establishes what would happen if someone broke a law in one state and then moved to another state. The judicial system of each state involved is required to work together to bring the defendant to justice. This clause also makes it possible to drive your car with your own state's driver's license in your wallet and not get arrested for illegally operating a motor vehicle in another state. Each state is required to recognize the validity of the other state's driver's licenses and other state-issued licenses.

This portion of the Constitution includes Article 4, Section 2, Clauses 2, also called the Extradition Clause. This clause outlines what would happen if a criminal tried to seek refuge in another state. In 1861, the Supreme Court amended this law to cover cases where the state governors needed to refuse extradition when justice demanded it. Clause 1 of this section has come under no small amount of scrutiny and controversy through the years. Originally, the clause was written to protect citizens traveling between states, but over the years, it has been subjected to four main interpretations.

Chapter 17

The first view says that the Founding Fathers intended this clause to be a restriction on Congress' discrimination against certain states. Today, this view has been declared constitutionally invalid. The second view says that this clause guarantees the citizens of one state could enjoy the same exact rights as another state. This view was rejected by the Supreme Court over a century ago. The third view says the clause ensures that all citizens have the right to exercise their own state's rights while visiting another state. This view was also rejected by the Supreme Court. The fourth view is rightly upheld by the Supreme Court and says this clause prohibits discrimination against citizens from other states. For example, someone who lives in one state can buy and sell property in another state.

Also important is how Article 4, Section 3, Clauses 1 and 2 protects the states from being divided into smaller states or being joined with another state to serve the interest or need of an elected official. Aren't you relieved to know that your congressmen can't divide or add onto your state? Again, this is an example of the checks and balances the Founding Fathers wrote into our Constitution.

Throughout the history of our country, this rule has been broken several times. One example was during the Civil War when West Virginia did not want to join Virginia in seceding from the Union. This revolt ended when the representatives of the the rebelling counties gathered in Wheeling, Virginia and decided to form a new state: West Virginia.

Along with being protected against alterations to our borders, each state has protection against being made into a separate government. Imagine what it would be like to always be concerned about an elected official turning your state into a socialist mini-country! Article 4, Section 4 establishes these guidelines. Individual states are mandated to follow the same rules the country as a whole has to follow, therefore making all of the states, and hence the country, a "Republic Form of Government." This article also mandated the federal government to protect each of the individual states from foreign attack as well as uprisings and insurrections.

We will be studying the amendments to the Constitution in coming chapters, but for now, let's take a look at *how* an amendment to the Constitution is made. The amendment process is yet another amazing - indeed, almost miraculous - feature of the Constitution.

Chapter 17

Our Founding Fathers knew that even though they had worked hard to construct our founding document, it would not be perfect. It was because of this awareness, they built in the ability to change the Constitution. They knew that if they made it too easy to amend, anyone could change it to suit their interests. Yet, if it was impossible to change, the Constitution would be oppressive to our country.

To amend the Constitution, a formal process has to be strictly followed. First, a proposed amendment must be brought to both of the houses of Congress by a two-thirds vote. Next, it needs to be ratified by three-fourths of the state legislatures or the same number of state constitutional conventions. As you can see, this is a difficult, but not impossible process to complete. There have been twenty-seven amendments made to the Constitution.

So, what can we do as citizens of this great country, to protect our Constitution? First and foremost, we must *know the Constitution* to be able to protect it. How well do you know it?

In the words of the Framers...

James Madison

"This may be rendered a very convenient instrument of justice and be particularly beneficial on the borders of contiguous states."

"If the Constitution was not the supreme law, other laws would arise in conflict to the Constitution, thus leading citizens in all different directions, creating a monster, in which the head was under to direction of the members."

Chapter 17

So what happened after the Constitution was written, signed, and ratified?

Although the new government was established and accepted by enough states for ratification, other world nations were not convinced of its strength. Great European powers doubted the young United States could protect itself against bullies. Although the United States had joined the French in 1778 in the Treaty of Alliance and trade pact, President George Washington was being pressured to denounce both.

Washington resolved to remain neutral, and on April 22, 1793, he issued his Neutrality Proclamation. This proclamation urged Americans to remain impartial toward all possible foreign foe and to not engage in any actions that would show the country's involvement in foreign wars. At this time, the French Revolution had rocked France, and England and France were involved in yet another war.

A young French diplomat, named Edmond Charles Genét came to Charleston, South Carolina with the goal of setting up a base for French operations against Spain and England, This instigating, young French man tried to hire war veterans to fight Spanish owned Florida and Louisiana. When President Washington refused to listen to him, Genét announced that he would go over Washington's head and appeal to the American people themselves. Genét caused quite the stir before Washington finally got Secretary of State Jefferson's support and had Genét removed from the country. Congress then passed laws to keep this type of trouble from happening again.

This incident marked the end of Thomas Jefferson's career as Secretary of State. These early years of our nation's history were rather tumultuous. One trial after another faced our first president. After the Neutrality Proclamation, Washington also dealt with the issues that arose over the waterways. The United States was working hard to establish their identity as a world trade power, but Britain especially did not want to yield waterways.

Chapter 17

British ship crews were sick and tired of low pay and poor treatment. They took every opportunity to desert the British ships to join the American shipping industry. Of course this made the British angry, and in response, they seized American ships, forcing the crew to serve them. This practice was called impressment.

President Washington did not want to go to war with Britain again. He knew that if America could not have some years of peace, it would never grow strong enough to survive. He appointed John Jay to head a peace mission with Great Britain. The treaty that was put into place was not popular with the American people, but war was sidestepped for a little longer. The issues with Britain were not completely settled until the War of 1812.

Meanwhile, Washington was also dealing with the unsettling presence of Spanish forts in the southern, American frontier regions. The president responded by sending Thomas Pinckney to Spain to make a treaty with Spain. In 1795, a treaty was made, making the 31st parallel of latitude the southern boundary of the United States of America.

Washington was followed by John Adams as president. Adams had his own presidential issues to deal with! When he came to office, the British were still seizing American ships, but the greatest problem was the French, who were angry about the Jay Treaty with Britain. President Adams was able to avoid outright war with France, although there were hostilities between the two countries.

John Adams

In 1799, when Napoleon Bonaparte became the ruler of France, he was nervous about the strength of the young United States. He was eager to settle the two countries' differences by signing a new agreement called the Convention of 1800.

Chapter 17

Would you like to know more about this time period? You might like to research the Alien and Sedition Acts. What were they? Who tried to put them into place? Why?

Stretching and Growing

1790 - 1860

Chapter 18: Our Changing Country

Chapter 19: The War of 1812 & the Jacksonian Period

Chapter 20: America Grows and Changes

Please Leave Blank.

Chapter 18 — Our Changing Country

There is nothing easy about keeping a nation united and running the way it is supposed to! There have always been arguments and disagreements about how best to do this. From the beginning of our country, there have been political parties. The first were the Federalists and the Republican (also called the Republican/Democratic) parties.

The election of 1800 was monumental in many ways. Even though the Federalists didn't care for John Adams, they chose him to run for re-election with Charles Cotesworth Pinckney as his vice-president. The Republicans chose Thomas Jefferson as their candidate, along with Aaron Burr as the vice-presidential candidate.

The ballots did not state which man was running for which office, and this caused a great deal of confusion. This had not been the first time this omission had caused issues for the voters. In 1796, the same problem had occurred. When the votes of the 1800 election were counted, Jefferson and Burr received the same number of votes. Both of them received more votes than John Adams and Charles Pinckney. As you learned when you studied the Constitution, in the case of a tie, the president would be selected by the House of Representatives. Each state would have one vote, and the winner would be whomever received the most votes.

At this point, Aaron Burr refused to defer to Jefferson. He would not admit that he was really running for the office of vice-president. Finally, after thirty-six ballots, Thomas Jefferson was finally named third president of the United States of America.

As president, Thomas Jefferson knew that he needed to be careful whom he replaced from the previous administrations. He ousted only those Federalists who had acted contrary to the good of the country. He allowed the Alien and Sedition Acts to expire, and he pardoned those jailed under the act as well. He and his secretary of the treasury were able to cut the nation's debt by half, which in turn, allowed him to abolish the whiskey tax - a move which increased his popularity.

Chapter 18

Throughout his presidency, Thomas Jefferson learned to be less judgmental of others in office, realizing that it is indeed a difficult task to be a truly consistent politician. One of the challenges Thomas Jefferson faced as president came from the small countries in North Africa. These Muslim countries, known as the Barbary States, were charging a tribute from ships that sailed on the Mediterranean Sea. While he had held the office of Secretary of State, Jefferson had suggested a campaign to organize an international blockade to break up the piracy system. Nothing had come of this plan, though, and the pirates continued to collect their two million dollar per year fee from the United States.

When the bold Barbary pirates raised their fee, President Jefferson refused to pay it. The pasha of Tripoli declared war, and President Jefferson sent armed forces to the area to protect American interests and to deal with the terrorists. Commodores Richard Dale and Stephen Decatur were in charge of American operations there. The North Africans seized the American frigate, *Philadelphia*, and ran it aground. Rather then let Tripoli have the ship, Commodore Decatur sneaked into the terrorists' territory and burned it.

Finally, in 1815, a combined British-American force moved in on the pirates, breaking up their ring once and for all, and breaking the back of the piracy ring. This skirmish, which became known as the Tripolitan War, served to show the world that America was not someone to mess with. The United States was starting to gain respect as a nation.

In the year 1800, the port of New Orleans was extremely important to the United States, especially to those settlements west of the Appalachian Mountains. Almost half of all American trade passed through this port in Spanish-owned Louisiana Territory. It was in 1800 that Spain ceded this territory back to its original owner, France.

President Jefferson accurately observed that the French ruler, Napoleon Bonaparte was planning a New World empire. Napoleon, who had been forced into a truce with Britain, was itching to expand French holdings in the New World. Napoleon ordered his brother-in-law, Charles LeClerk, and an enormous number of troops to land in Haiti, a convenient location from which to attack North America. At the same time, Napoleon stationed troops in Holland, ordering them to be ready to sail across the Atlantic and attack North America from the east.

Chapter 18

President Jefferson was aware of all of this activity, and after weighing his options, he decided to try to purchase New Orleans, as well as place the country on high alert. As he prepared for what appeared to be imminent battle, Jefferson worked on Napoleon. These two men were truly engaged in a battle of wit; both of them were highly intelligent and equally motivated to further the futures of their countries.

As Providence would have it, Napoleon never did have a chance to attack and conquer North America. A series of unfortunate (for him!) events occurred, and Napoleon was forced to reconsider his plans. First, his troops in Haiti suffered heavy loss in a Yellow Fever epidemic, which swept through the island. His troops in Holland suffered from severe weather that stranded them far from home and made it impossible to sail across the Atlantic Ocean to attack the eastern coast of North America.

President Jefferson observed these events and leveled the final blow. He declared that he did not want the Louisiana Territory after all. Even though he and Napoleon had been dickering over prices for quite some time, Jefferson now acted as if he wanted to walk away from the bargaining table. He declared that purchasing the territory would divide the country into eastern and western sections and therefore would be hard to unite. Of course, this was another round of their battle of wits, but Napoleon decided to believe Jefferson.

After Jefferson's bluff, Napoleon decided that he needed to focus his attention on defeating Britain once and for all. His great North American empire would just have to wait - he figured he could always conquer the United States later. To defeat Britain, though, Napoleon needed money! He thought if he could get Jefferson to purchase the entire Louisiana Territory, it would serve two purposes: he would have the money he needed, and he could deal with a "divided" America later. In May of 1803, Thomas Jefferson nearly doubled the size of the United States by purchasing the Louisiana Territory for fifteen million dollars, which is about 2.8 cents an acre.

With one signature, the United States owned hundreds of square miles of unmapped wilderness. President Jefferson was highly interested in learning more about the West, and he knew just the man to lead an exploration. He hired his friend and private secretary, Meriwether Lewis, to lead the first of two exploration expeditions into the new territory. Lewis

Chapter 18

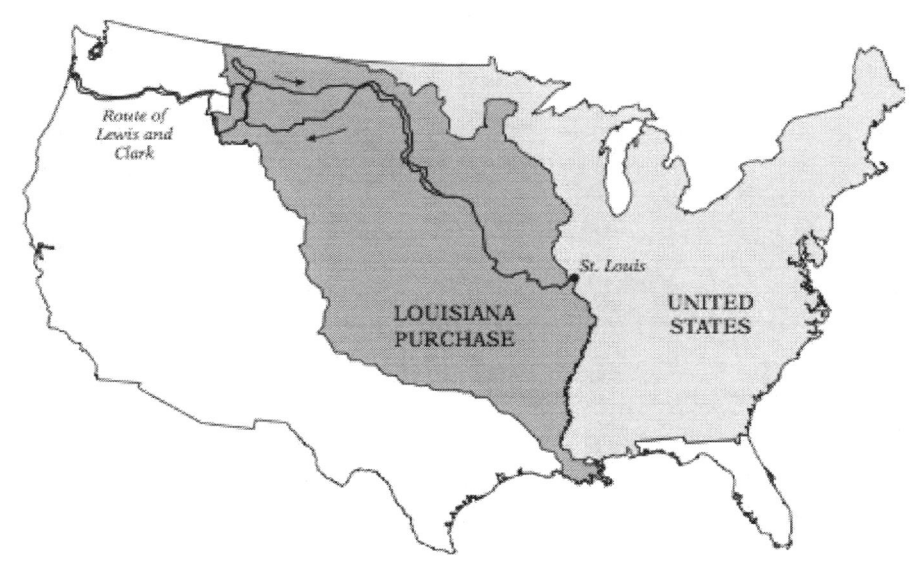

chose William Clark, his former commanding officer in the Indian Wars in the Northwest territory, to help him lead the expedition.

On May 14, 1804, twenty-nine explorers, along with seven soldiers, nine river-men, and Captain Clark's personal slave, York, set out on the grand adventure. The expedition took two years and four months to complete. Lewis and Clark made maps and collected specimens of nature all along the way. Their detailed journal entries showed the "new" flora and fauna discovered in the territory. On their return, Lewis and Clark were celebrities. Their journey had opened the eyes of many easterners and fueled the interest of those wanting to travel west. The group had found the Western Native Americans to be friendly for the most part, and curious, with no reason to be overly suspicious of these white explorers. Unfortunately, it would only be a few years before these same natives would have reason to be very suspicious of the white people.

The second expedition, which occurred in two parts, was called the Pike Expedition because Zebulon Pike led it. In 1805, on the first part of the Pike Expedition, Pike followed the Mississippi River in search of its source. On Pike's second trip, in 1806-07, he traveled up the Arkansas River into Spanish-held territories, explored the Rocky Mountains, and explored the Rio Grande on his return trip. While he was in the Rockies, he spotted the peak that would be named after him, Pike's Peak.

During Thomas Jefferson's second term in office, he dealt with more issues with British and French ships raiding and impressing American sailors. Through a trade embargo, which cut trading with both offending countries and infuriated many American merchants, an agreement was eventually reached, and war was again postponed. When our fourth

Chapter 18

president, James Madison, was elected in 1809, Congress had finally relented concerning the trading embargo. They decided that America would trade with Britain and France if those countries ceased attacking American ships.

Napoleon responded by lifting his country's bands on American trade goods (these were the Berlin and Milan Decrees), but in the same day, he signed a new decree that confiscated all of the American ships in French trade ports. America chose to ignore his insulting actions and began trading with the French again.

By early 1810, there were more Indian uprisings against settlements on the western Indian Territory. The unfair treatment and broken promises of the American government against the Native Americans had finally caught up with them. The Indians were no longer willing to give up their land and lashed out in anger. They brought their tribes together to form an Indian confederation under the leadership of Tecumseh, a Shawnee Chief. There seemed to be many issues that needed to be addressed. President James Madison had his hands full and many decisions to make.

Chapter 19 — The War of 1812 & the Jacksonian Period

Section 1:

When the United States purchased the Louisiana Territory for the United States, we bought land, which was the home of thousands of people. Nearly fifty thousand French and Spanish Creoles lived in the territory. Did the American purchase of this territory automatically make these people citizens of the United States? What about the British who still occupied their pre-Revolutionary period forts? These forts dotted the West and posed a rising problem to the growing United States.

With the British making life miserable for the American sailors, and the occupants of the forts tormenting the pioneers in the West, it was becoming abundantly clear that they were becoming more than a nuisance. When the Indian Confederation began to work with the British soldiers in the Western forts against the settlers and travelers, Americans became extremely angry. Throughout 1811 and 1812, relations with Britain deteriorated even more, until America finally declared war on Britain. This war lasted two and a half years and would become known as the War of 1812.

Section 2:

Between the years of James Monroe's presidency through the 1820s, America saw the purchase of Florida, revolutions in Central America, and the presidencies of James Monroe and John Quincy Adams. It was also the years of the Monroe Doctrine and the Missouri Compromise. Let's take a closer look at each of these events.

Spanish-owned Florida had been facing difficulties for quite some time. Spain had been losing control of the region. The citizens living along the western border of Florida revolted against the Spanish and asked to become part of the United States. Other Florida citizens moved north into Mississippi and Alabama, and soon both territories had enough people to become states and join the Union.

Chapter 19

Slaves from southern states ran away to Florida by the thousands. Many of them joined forces with Floridian Seminole Indians. Together they frequently crossed over the border and attacked unprotected American settlements. Secretary of State Adams demanded that the Spanish do something to control what was happening in Florida. When the Spanish refused to do anything, Secretary of War Calhoun gave General Andrew Jackson control of the Georgia and Tennessee state militias.

Andrew Jackson pushed his orders further than intended and invaded Florida, surprising the Indians and disposing of the Spanish government. When the United States government refused to pay for the damages or reprimand Jackson for his actions, Spain decided it would be better off selling Florida. They didn't have the funds or soldiers for a war over it. In 1819, the United States made a treaty and purchased East Florida for five million dollars, along with an agreement that America would keep the lands in West Florida that had been conquered by Andrew Jackson.

Meanwhile, in Central America, Mexico was fighting to throw off the Spanish rule. Napoleon Bonaparte had named his brother, Joseph, the king of Spain in 1808. The Spanish American colonists had no loyalty to this new king and wanted to rid themselves of his rule. The Spanish social scale placed Spanish-born settlers at the top of the scale of importance. The Creoles, those citizens born in Latin America but of European descent, were thought to be inferior.

The Creoles were educated, and many were wealthy. This meant they had the ability and the means to take action in leadership positions. The Creoles disliked Spanish control of their economy. The Mestizos - those who were half European and half Indian - were thought to be lower than the Creoles. The Mestizos, Indians, and blacks were in favor of the Creoles, because they favored ridding themselves of the Spanish rule completely. None of them thought it was fair that Spain got the profits that they themselves should be receiving.

Two influential Creoles, José de San Martín in the south and Simón Bolívar in the north, led revolts and threw off the Spanish government. Their efforts were somewhat in vain, however. Their effort to create a republic modeled after the government of the United States fell flat because of the poor economic conditions and high illiteracy rate. The people were

Chapter 19

used to being ruled by an autocracy, and the Catholic Church had a strong grip. When chaos broke out, it was the perfect chance for strong military leaders to take control. President Monroe looked on in concern. Would strong, foreign powers try to intervene? If they did interfere with the chaos in the south, what would be the next step? Would the United States have to fight off foreign powers trying to build colonies on their land?

President Monroe was especially concerned about Russia. Alaska had long been one of Russia's most profitable fur trading territories, and now they had begun to move down the coast. They had build a fort just to the north of San Francisco by the year 1812, and by 1821, they had claimed the land along the Pacific Coast of Canada. Some of this land had already been claimed by both Britain and the United States.

All of this activity made President Monroe extremely nervous. He felt like the United States was being squeezed on all sides. When he heard that the French were planning to send shiploads of troops to Latin America, he asked Thomas Jefferson, James Madison, and John Quincy Adams to come to the capitol to help him figure out the situation. Lord George Canning, the British Foreign Secretary, had contacted President Monroe, requesting that the United States agree to issue a joint declaration to warn other European nations to stay of North America.

Monroe told Adams, "When a 'weak' nation accepts partnership with a stronger, she places herself at the mercy of her ally." President Monroe had decided with the helpful advice of his friends, to issue an independent declaration, separate from Britain. John Quincy Adams wrote up the statement for his friend, the president, and on December 2, 1823, Monroe included it in his annual message to the Congress. This statement would become known as the Monroe Doctrine.

The Monroe Doctrine added three important principles to the United States foreign policy. It was, in essence, a declaration to the rest of the world that "the American continents… [were] not to be considered as subjects of future colonization by any European powers." Secondly, it stated that the United States would not become involved or interfere with European affairs or wars unless its rights were "invaded or seriously menaced." If and when that happened, it would "make preparations for [its] defense." Thirdly, the statement

Chapter 19

declared that the United States "should consider any attempt…to extend their system to any portion of our hemisphere as dangerous to [its] space and safety as well" as an unfriendly act. To summarize the statement, the United States prohibited European meddling in the western hemisphere's business, while promising to not get involved unnecessarily with European affairs. The Monroe Doctrine served its purpose well, and in the future, it became one of the most important parts of American foreign policy.

America was not only dealing with foreign threats; there was a major issue right here in our midst that threatened to snuff out the fires of freedom and equality. When our Founders had crafted the Constitution, they did not address the long-term effects that slavery would have on our country and on our society. Perhaps they felt they would address it later, or maybe they felt pressured to leave it alone in order to gain the approval needed from the states in order to gain ratification. At any rate, with the country growing in leaps and bounds, the issue of slavery *had* to be addressed. The original Northern states had abolished or were in the process of abolishing slavery. The states formed out of the Northwest Territory had never allowed slavery, but the Southern states, where slavery had originally spread, still had many captive blacks.

In 1819, there were twenty-two states in the Union - eleven were free states, and eleven were slave states. America was growing in the westward direction, and Missouri wanted to be granted statehood as a slave state; however, this created a problem - more slave states than free states. The balance would be upset. As of yet, the slavery argument was not a moral one, but mostly economic and political.

A compromise was reached when Maine applied for statehood as a free-state. Missouri would be allowed to come into the Union as a slave state, and the balance would be maintained. This compromise settled an argument for the short-term, but it didn't settle the long-term problem. What would happen in the future when all of the lands acquired in the Louisiana Purchase applied for statehood? What about Florida? What if Texas gained independence from Mexico and applied for statehood? What if slaveholders moved from a slave state to a free state? Could they take their slaves with them? And what about our government; could they decide to make slavery in any state illegal? There were a whole slew

Chapter 19

of questions concerning slavery flying around. The impasse was finally worked out by Henry Clay of Kentucky, who suggested a plan that would be called the Missouri Compromise. A balance of free and slave states had to be maintained, and slavery would be forbidden north of 36° 30' north latitude. As we will see in coming chapters, this compromise did not settle any of the underlying issues, which were plaguing our country.

Chapter 20 — America Grows and Changes

This chapter is written in a slightly different style than the other chapters in this book. There were so many events during this time period that I find it impossible to dig deeply into each one. In order to maintain the flow of our story, I have laid out the most important events on a timeline for you to study.

In our last chapter's deep research assignments, you discovered how Andrew Jackson, our seventh president, removed the Cherokees, among other Indian nations. This was an extremely tumultuous time in our country's history, yet it was also a time of growth and invention. Our timeline is going to back up just a bit to 1817, because something monumental happened that year.

Timeline of Events from 1817 - 1857

1817 - The construction of the Erie Canal begins. DeWitt Clinton headed up the construction of this amazing canal. This hand-dug canal connected Albany, New York, on the Hudson River to Lake Erie. The original canal included an astounding system of locks, which "stepped" the boats up to Lake Erie. The Canal opened for business in 1825

1819 - The Missouri Compromise postpones the inevitable decision concerning the future of slavery.
- The purchase of Florida settles the issues with Spain.

1823 - The Monroe Doctrine proclaimed as America's new foreign policy.

Chapter 20

1800-1825 - The Second Great Awakening swept the nation. As America grew in land holdings and in population, so did a spiritual awakening. Camp meetings were popular as thousands of people gathered to sing and listen to traveling ministers. The Awakening energized churches across the nation to become involved with cultural issues facing our country. Social activism birthed abolition groups, temperance and suffrage societies, and prison ministries. Among the most notable evangelists and abolitionists was Charles G. Finney. This Second Great Awakening had many long-lasting positive effects on our nation.

1828 - The "Tariff of Abominations" is put into place by Congress, triggering a domino effect of higher cost and decreased trade with foreign nations.

1832 - The Black Hawk War was actually an attack on about four hundred Indians, who were not posing a threat. Settlers panicked and called the army to trap and kill the group. Black Hawk, the leader of the group, escaped only to be turned over to the authorities by a band of Winnebago Indians.

1836 - The siege of the Alamo… Americans, who had been allowed to immigrate into Texas, held by Mexico, had become too strong and independent for the Mexican government. Eventually, the Texans declared independence from Mexico, and war began. A group of 183 men barricaded themselves inside an old Spanish mission called the Alamo. They didn't stand a chance as the Mexican general, Santa Anna, laid siege on the Alamo. Every single person inside the old mission was killed, including Jim Bowie, the creator of the famous Bowie knife, and Davy Crockett, a backwoodsman and senator from Tennessee. Texas eventually won its freedom and the battle cry, "Remember the Alamo!" still rings through history. Texas became a state in 1845.

Chapter 20

1844 — Samuel Morse demonstrates the telegraph. The telegraph was invented to help the railroads run more smoothly. By stopping and starting electrical pulses, Morse could send messages over long distances through a copper wire. "What hath God wrought!" was the first message Morse sent through the telegraph.

1846-1848 — The Mexican War started only three weeks after our eleventh president, James K. Polk, took office. This war was not nationally popular, with many northerners believing that it had been carefully planned by the South, to gain more land and therefore more slave states. General Zachary Taylor gained hero status for his role in the war, much to President Polk's chagrin. (He was afraid that Taylor would want to replace him at the White House at the next election.) The Treaty of Guadalupe Hidalgo ended the war and made the Rio Grande the boundary of Texas. Five years after the end of the war, the United States purchased another section of land called the Gadsden Purchase.

1840-1850 — The far western lands of Oregon and California were opened up to settlement. There was a great rush of Americans who saw great opportunity awaiting them there.

1848 — On January 24, 1848, gold was discovered in a creek at Sutter's Fort. John Sutter, an immigrant from Switzerland was responsible for starting the California Gold Rush. By the fall of 1849, there were enough Californians to write their own state constitution. California asked to join the Union as a free state, therefore upsetting the balance of free/slave states. Because of this, Congress delayed granting their request until September 1850, when the Compromise of 1850 was passed.

Chapter 20

1850 - The Compromise of 1850 stated that California could enter the Union as a free state, but the lands gained through the Mexican cession were to be divided into two territories, New Mexico and Utah. Each of these territories would be allowed to vote on whether or not they could be slave or free states. The compromise also stated that there would be stricter laws concerning runaway slaves; it stated that all federal officials had to help return these slaves to their owners. This compromise made many Americans, who were starting to realize the evils of the slave practice, very angry and sad. It seemed that the U.S. government was trying to please the slave states more than govern justly.

1852 - *Uncle Tom's Cabin* was published. (We will learn more about this extremely important literary work in our next chapter.)

1854 - The Kansas-Nebraska Act declared that the western territories could decide for themselves whether they would be slave or free states. Of course this compromise did absolutely nothing to solve the real problem. After the Kansas-Nebraska Act was passed, both free and slave advocates rushed to the West. The two sides clashed badly, and soon, the area was called "Bleeding Kansas." The bloodshed and violence there was only a prelude of what was soon to happen nationwide.

1857 - The Dred Scott decision. (You will research this history-making event in your student journal work.)

United We Stand

1860 - 1900

Chapter 21: A Country Divided

Chapter 22: The War Between the States Part 1

Chapter 23: The War Between the States Part 2

Chapter 24: Reconstruction

Chapter 25: The Big Business Boom

Chapter 26: The Turn of the Century

Please leave blank.

Chapter 21 — A Country Divided

By the year 1850, America had grown in astounding ways. The population had reached thirty-one million, and prosperity was widespread. God had blessed this land with resources only dreamed about in many other nations around the world. The land and wilderness, navigable rivers, abundant wildlife, and trees would allow our land to enjoy progress in future generations also. Despite the progress and abundance, however, our country was facing problems which were quite capable of tearing us in two. Would our young nation survive? Would we be strong and progressive people on the other side of this tangle?

In this chapter we are going to explore the decade leading up to the great, civil war that would rend our country's heart and soul. First, let us take a better look at what exactly separated the North and the South. There were several issues that led the nation down the road to war. These were not new issues, but they were being widely noticed and paid attention to for the first time in our history. For years, compromises had held off the inevitable fight, but by the mid to late 1850s, there was no more room or desire to continue this facade.

There were differences between the North and the South, which made it difficult to see eye to eye on many different issues. The South was largely agricultural. It was the South that produced most of the nation's crops, both for consumption and for sale. The South also did not have many large cities, and the cities they did have centered around agricultural trade. New Orleans was the largest Southern city, with a population of 150,000. The Southern upper class, which was about one percent of the entire population, were plantation owners who generally owned a large number of slaves. It was this upper class that were the rulers of the South, socially and economically.

In contrast to this, the North was industrialized. Where the South had huge plantations worked by thousands of slaves, the North had factories operated by the many poor and "lower class" citizens. The North's great cities, many with large populations, were crowded and noisy. By the 1850s, New York had a population of well over 800,000 people. Thanks to the huge boom of immigration, which brought three million people to the country, the North's population soared. It is estimated that seven out of eight of these immigrants settled in the North or headed West. Although the South was built by the sweat of the African slaves, a vast amount of the North's industry was operated by the men, women, and even children of the lowest class. These factory workers' hours were extremely long and the work was grueling.

Slowly but surely, these hard-working immigrants bettered their living standard and stepped into positions of leadership in politics. These elected officials were sensitive to the needs and desires of their fellow immigrants. In New York, Philadelphia, and Boston, Irish voters were extremely influential in elections. In the Midwest cities, Milwaukee, St. Louis, and Cincinnati, the German influence was strong.

These vastly different lifestyles and economics produced differing political opinions and views as well. Northerners, as a general rule, were more in favor of a strong federal government. Their larger population was able to pay the larger amount of taxes required to have more governmental programs. Because of this, the North had more schools and higher education rates.

In contrast, many Southerners were afraid of a strong central government. They held strongly to what Thomas Jefferson believed: the ideal government is local and state government. You might say that the majority of the Southerners of the mid-nineteenth century were Antifederalists. The South held the view that education was a private issue and therefore had nothing to do with the federal government. As a result, there were fewer schools, because most Southerners would not pay taxes for government-run schools.

As you can see, the North and South disagreed sharply about almost everything. The South, knowing they were in the minority, held tenaciously to their way of life and glared in defiance at the bigger, stronger North.

Last, but certainly not least, the view of slavery divided the country more than any other issue between them. Slavery has been around almost as long as the human race has

Chapter 21

been in existence, so why was it such a big deal here in America? I think we all know that one of the big issues with slavery in this country lies in the fact that we believe that "all men [humans] are created equal."

Another issue with slavery here in America was the fact that slavery was limited to one race of people, the black people. Also disturbing was the insanely profitable business slave traders ran, buying and selling these stolen African citizens. By this time in our history, there were slaves being bought and sold, who were descendants of slaves brought here in the 1600s. Generation after generation of slaves were born, lived, and died in captivity. Many slave owners viewed their slaves no differently than their horse or dog. They had been taught for generations that the black slaves were no different than "any other animal." Some even took it so far as to believe that they, the slave owners, were doing a noble deed by "giving" the slaves a place to live and work to do. There were plenty of Americans who were tired of compromising and looking the other direction; this atrocity needed to end.

Most northerners had no comprehension of what a slave's life was like, but there were some who made it their business to find out. Many of these Northerners helped the slaves to find freedom by providing them shelter and helping on their flight to freedom. All over the nation, a huge network of "safe houses" gave the runaway slaves a place of safety and rest on their dangerous, and potentially deadly, journey north. This network of people was called the Underground Railroad. When the Fugitive Slave Law of 1850 was passed, the Underground Railroad responded by broadening its borders all the way up into Canada.

Some black people, who made it to freedom before the Fugitive Slave Law, were gaining attention for the anti-slave cause by speaking out about the condition in which the slaves lived. Frederick Douglass and Harriet Tubman were two of the leading black abolitionists.

Frederick Douglass wrote and spoke about the horrors of slavery. He used the money he earned from the sale of his book to help other escaped slaves. If you would like to read Frederick Douglass' book, *The Narrative of the Life of Frederick Douglass*, it is still available. Harriet Tubman returned time and again to help rescue her friends and family from slavery,

Chapter 21

earning the name "Moses" for her bravery. During her rescue missions, Harriet worked with the Underground Railroad to deliver about three hundred slaves to freedom.

In 1852, the plight of runaway slaves and the life they endured in captivity was brought to the public's attention in a unique and quite wonderful way. Harriet Beecher Stowe, the daughter of a preacher and the mother of seven children, wrote and published a book that spun the nation on its ear. Harriet Beecher Stowe had lost a young son to cholera in the year 1849, and because of this experience, she wanted to share what it felt like to lose a child. The Stowe family lived in Cincinnati, Ohio, right across the Ohio River from Kentucky, a slave state. Mrs. Stowe had watched the happenings of the slave trade. She imagined that the slave mothers felt like she had felt at the death of her son, when their children were taken away and sold to someone else.

In 1850, Mrs. Stowe began writing a story, which was published in installments in the National Era, an anti-slavery newspaper. In 1851, the complete story was published in book form. *Life Among the Lowly,* also known as *Uncle Tom's Cabin,* became an almost instant hit, selling three hundred thousand copies in one year.

Uncle Tom's Cabin is one of the most influential pieces of literature in American history. The book served to stir the hearts of those waking up to the evils of slavery. *Uncle Tom's Cabin* deeply affected a tall lawyer from Illinois, who had his eye on the White House. Abraham Lincoln was not an abolitionist, but he was opposed to the spread of slavery. His main concern was preserving the Union, and when the Democratic party split over the choice of their candidate, the Republicans decided Lincoln was their best choice. The South did not see Lincoln as their friend and declared that, if he won the election of 1860, they would leave the Union.

Chapter 22 — The War Between the States
Part 1

The Presidential election of 1860 was a crucial decision in our nation. The Southern extremists, called "fire-eaters," threatened to leave the Union if the anti-slave Republicans won. The Democratic party was split in the North/South direction when Illinois senator, Stephen Douglas, won the nomination. Douglas was a moderate, but the fire-eaters refused to stand behind him. Instead, they withdrew from the convention and nominated their own candidate, John C. Breckenridge of Kentucky. This split in the Democratic Party gave the Republicans an edge in the presidential race.

The border states, Delaware, Maryland, Virginia, and Kentucky, did not support the South's decision to leave the Union. They believed if they could buy some time, the fire-eaters would see that there could not be any good, long-lasting results from their secession. To buy some time, these border states selected their own candidate and formed their own party, the Constitutional Union Party. Their candidate, John Bell, stood for staying in the Union.

In the election, Lincoln carried most of the votes, with Douglas coming in second, followed by Breckenridge and Bell. However, Lincoln had not won a single Southern state, which put him at an extreme disadvantage. How could he convince the South not to leave the Union when they did not want him to be the president?

President Buchanan was still in office when South Carolina voted to leave the Union. The president did nothing to stop them; he decided to let Lincoln deal with them. Before

Chapter 22

Abraham Lincoln took office, Florida, Mississippi, Alabama, Georgia, Louisiana, and Texas all followed North Carolina's lead.

On February 1, 1861, delegates from these states met in Montgomery, Alabama to form their own union, the Confederate States of America. They wrote their own constitution and voted for their own president, Jefferson Davis. This was the condition of the country when Abraham Lincoln, our sixteenth president, took office.

The South felt that it had the right to withdraw from the Union, but President Lincoln did not agree. He believed that once a state had joined the Union, it was a permanent part of our country. This became the main reason for the Civil War - to determine which one would prevail. In his inaugural speech, President Lincoln told the nation that he would do everything he could to reconcile the country, but if he had to fight to preserve the Constitution and the Union, he would. He also promised that if it were required, he would use the power of government "to hold, occupy, and possess the property and places belonging to the government." This meant he would protect the federal forts located in the South - Fort Pickens at Pensacola, Florida, and Fort Sumter in Charleston's harbor, in South Carolina.

The South demanded that the North turn the control of these forts over to them. After all, they reasoned, the forts were located on the South's land. Of course, President Lincoln refused this demand. The South, knowing that the North could not hold the forts without supplies, refused the North access to them. The first fort to be tested was Fort Sumter.

Lincoln did not want the North to be the side that started the war. He reasoned that if the Confederates fired on Fort Sumter, they would be the ones who started the war. President Lincoln requested that a federal supply ship be allowed to bring supplies to the Northern officers and soldiers inside the fort. Confederate President Davis refused, and on April 12, 1861, when the ship tried to come through the harbor, the Confederate's opened fire on the fort. The South won the first battle of the Civil War when the Union troops inside Fort Sumter surrendered. They had endured forty hours of bombardment. All over the South, celebrations filled the streets.

Chapter 22

President Lincoln called for troops, and the border states were called upon to take sides. Virginia, Arkansas, and Tennessee all reluctantly joined the Confederacy. In all of the commotion, a new state was born. The citizens of fifty counties in western Virginia refused to join the rest of the state in their secession; they applied for statehood in the Union and became West Virginia in 1863.

Lincoln worked hard to keep the border states, and when the dust settled and the lines were drawn, the Union seemed to have a vast advantage over the South. The South did have a fighting chance, however. First, their goal was rather simple - to maintain control over their territory and set up an independent nation, the Confederate States of America. To accomplish this goal, they did not have to think about invading the North; they could stay in their home territory. Also, in their favor was the size of their territory. Even though the South was more sparsely populated, the mere size of the South would help to protect her. The North would have to stretch out long supply lines in order to reach their troops, the further south they invaded.

The second advantage the South held was the fact that the average citizen was extremely involved. Their way of life was being threatened, and they were willing to fight to protect it. Thirdly, the South was convinced that they could easily gain foreign aid. Since so many European countries had come to depend heavily on trade with the South, the Confederates believed they would garner their sympathy. Last, but not least, the South had a expansive coastline; it would take thousands of Northern ships to form a blockade off of the Southern coast.

In contrast, much of the North's advantage lay in their much larger industrial strength. Where the South had very few factories for manufacturing goods, the North had around 120,000 at the time of the Civil war. These factories enabled the North to produce their own war supplies, as well as the supplies of everyday life. The North's population was also much larger than the South's, and with about three hundred thousand immigrants arriving every year, it remained much more substantial throughout the war. Also, in the North's favor was their much larger navy.

Chapter 22

Throughout the country, families were divided by the war; brother fought against brother. In his passionate plea for the Union, President Lincoln used the words of Matthew 12:25, "A house divided against itself shall not stand." How would our country survive?

The battle at Fort Sumter in April of 1861 had thrown the country into a war craze. Young men from all over the nation were signing up to fight what they thought would be a short skirmish. Little did they know that this bloody war would rage on for four long years. At first, both sides relied completely on volunteers to fight, but as the volunteer numbers waned, both Presidents Lincoln and Davis began to draft men for their armies. The Union soldiers were often called "Billy Yanks" or "Yankees," and Confederate soldiers were called "Johnny Rebs" or "Rebels."

The war affected the South's economy in an extremely negative way. Counterfeit Confederate currency flooded the South, causing major inflation. Poor transportation methods made it difficult, and sometimes impossible, to get the goods to those who needed them. As the war raged on and more railroads were damaged, the situation became dire indeed. Hunger and poverty were widespread for many of the Southern citizens.

Many historians call the Civil War "The First Modern War." Railroads made it possible to move troops and supplies more quickly, and better guns, cannons, and methods of fighting were employed. Communications were also much more advanced than they had been in previous wars, as telegraph wires carried government orders to generals on the front lines. Ironclad ships were also used for the first time during the Civil War.

Even today, we can view images of the Civil War, thanks to the advances in photography at that time. Mathew Brady was one of the most well-known photographers of

Chapter 22

the Civil War. His photos covered many of the newspapers' front pages during the war. For the first time in history, many soldiers had photographs taken for their loved ones.

Let's take a look at the war strategies of both the North and of the South. The Union strategy had four main points of focus. First, they desired to impose a naval blockade with the goal to shut off as many supplies as possible to the South. This stranglehold would kill the economy of the South. Second, the Union knew they needed to control the Mississippi River; this would cut the South in half length-wise. The Mississippi River was also an important transportation route. The Union's third goal was to take Richmond, Virginia, which had become the Confederate's capital city. Lastly, the Union knew they needed to protect Washington D.C., their own capital.

The South's war strategy was extremely simple. Number one, they needed to break the naval blockade in order to receive supplies and aid from foreign countries. They also desperately needed to gain recognition from France and Britain as an independent nation.

One of the ways the Confederacy tried to achieve this was to cut off cotton trade with Britain in order to make them realize how much Britain needed the South's products. The Confederate's final strategy was to fight a defensive battle. They knew if any of their main cities fell to the Union, they would have a profoundly difficult time regaining control. They needed to stay in control of their territory all the way through the war.

After the battle at Fort Sumter, the North and South eyed each other warily. Eagerness to get the fighting underway was rising on both sides. Everyone's eyes were on Richmond, Virginia, the Confederate capital city, which lay a mere one hundred miles south of Washington D.C. In July of 1861, a Union force, under the leadership of General Irvin McDowell, marched on a Confederate force located at Manassas, Virginia, twenty miles south of Washington D.C. The Confederates heard of the Union's intentions and sent more troops to help those camped along Bull Run Creek near to Manassas. The Union army fought well, but they could not advance past the Confederate troops and their leader Thomas Jackson. This battle earned Jackson the nickname, "Stonewall Jackson," which followed him throughout the war.

Chapter 22

The battle turned into a panicked Union retreat, and the stunned North began to realize that this war was not going to be as short-lived as they initially believed it would be. The Confederates also realized that this war to establish their country was not going to be won overnight. Both sides also realized that their soldiers were not trained well enough.

President Lincoln placed George B. McClellan in charge of protecting Washington D.C. and training the troops. McClellan did an excellent job of turning the Northern army into a fighting machine. Meanwhile, in the South, the army was being trained and conditioned to face the war in front of them.

The armies met again when McClellan led the troops in a surprise attack in a less-guarded area between the James and York Rivers. McClellan could have won that battle, but he stalled, believing he should wait for more troops. Because of this pause in his attack, the Confederates had a chance to replace their wounded general. The replacing Confederate officer proved to be an issue for the Northern troops. General Robert E. Lee was a confident leader, a skilled general, and was extremely familiar with the area. Lee attacked McClellan and drove the Union army out of the area and back to Washington.

Confederate General Robert E. Lee

The North reeled from shock; could it be possible that the South could win? It seemed that every time the North sought to gain a foothold in the South, they were driven back. With every victory, the South gained confidence that they would gain their independence from the Union. Americans on both sides held their breath to see what would happen next.

Chapter 23 — The War Between the States
Part 2

The beginning of the Civil War was marked prominently by the South having the upper hand and gaining decisive victories - but would they be able to maintain their momentum? President Lincoln knew that if the Union was to win the war, they needed to cut off supplies to the South. The Union needed to establish a blockade along the coast to keep trade from getting through.

In order to have enough ships for a successful blockade, the Secretary of the Navy began buying up ships to build the fleet. Once the sea blockade was in place, they concentrated on ten major ports in the South. These ports were connected to the inland by railroads. Although the South was able to slip ships through the blockade, not nearly enough made it through to sustain the South completely. Eventually, the strain was too great for the South to bear. This blockade was largely responsible for breaking the Confederacy, even though it took four long years to accomplish it.

Another major area of attention for the North was the Mississippi River. This mighty river, which flows the length of our country, from Minnesota in the north to the Gulf of Mexico in the south, was not only a great way to divide the South, but it was also important in the transporting of troops and supplies. The side who controlled the Mighty Mississippi had a major advantage.

As the war in the East waged back and forth, and each side focused on capturing and protecting Richmond, the war in the West centered on the goal of gaining control of the Mississippi River. The North knew that if they could gain control of the river, they could separate Arkansas, Texas, and Louisiana from the rest of the Confederacy. The Union officer in charge of this part of the operation was Ulysses S. Grant.

General Grant believed that the Union's success west of the Appalachian Mountains depended almost solely on gaining control of the major rivers. The Tennessee River, along with the Cumberland River, empties into the Ohio River, which is fed by smaller tributaries,

Chapter 23

General Grant

eventually empties into the Mississippi River. General Grant concentrated his efforts on gaining control of this area of the Mississippi River system.

As Grant and his troops moved down along the Tennessee River, they captured Fort Henry and Fort Donelson - these two Confederate forts defended the upper Mississippi River. With the capture of Corinth in 1862, the Union gained control of the Upper Mississippi, along with access to the important southern locations. Next, the Union army turned their attention to gaining control of the southern part of the Mississippi River. David Glasgow Farragut, a naval officer, and General Benjamin Butler, a land force officer, led the campaign to take New Orleans at the southern end of the river.

The Confederates controlled the river from two forts on a peninsula. One of their tactics was to stretch a huge chain across the river, only lifting it to allow Confederate boats to pass. Farragut and Butler knew they had to get through this blockade. In the darkness of night, they sent an advance party to unhook the chain, allowing the Union troops to stealthily slip past the forts. The Confederates in the forts realized what was going on and opened fire on the Union troops, but it was too late.

The Union army disabled and scattered the Confederate forces, and two days later, they took New Orleans. With Butler's troops occupying New Orleans, Farragut moved the Navy up the river, capturing first Baton Rouge, Louisiana, and then Nachez, Mississippi. By mid-summer 1863, the Union had complete control of the Mississippi River, except for one Confederate outpost, Vicksburg. Built high on a bluff above the Mississippi River, Vicksburg had beaten back Union troops six times, as they attempted to attack the town. Confederate general John C. Pemberton had inflicted heavy Union casualties as he repelled the Northern forces.

Chapter 23

General Grant ordered his forces to take only the supplies they could carry and come at Vicksburg from another direction. Grant moved his troops to cut the railroad access to Vicksburg. When Pemberton moved to cut off Grant's supply line, he was shocked to find there was none. By the time the Confederate troops made it back to Vicksburg, they were trapped with no escape route. The Union troops fired on Vicksburg around the clock for six weeks straight. With no food and no way to escape, the Confederates were forced to surrender Vicksburg. It had taken a year and a half, but Grant had gained control of the entire Mississippi River. It was July 4, 1863.

Meanwhile, in the East, Confederate General Lee decided to turn his strategy from defense to offense. His goal was to free Maryland from the Union's control. Doing this would also allow Southern farmers to harvest their crops with limited Union interference. Lee also hoped to gain Britain's assistance by showing that the South could not just defend their own ground, but could also take Union territory.

Through an amazing Union discovery of a lost Confederate dispatch outlining Lee's intentions, Union general McClellan made huge attacks on Lee's lines at Antietam. In one awful day, there were three battles fought. In the end, Lee and his troops retreated across the Potomac back into Virginia. Neither side called it a victory.

In December of 1862, the Union failed to dislodge the Confederate occupying Fredericksburg, and lost twice as many men as the Confederates. Union morale sank to an all time low. President Lincoln was still on the lookout for a general who could consistently win battles in the East. None of the leaders he had appointed had been able to strike fear in the hearts of the Confederates. It was at this point that President Lincoln called in "Fighting Joe" Hooker.

General Hooker confidently took 130,000 soldiers to meet up with General Lee's 60,000 soldiers near a town called Chancellorsville. Lee knew Hooker was coming, and because he was extremely familiar with the area, he took the Union soldiers by surprise. What followed is considered to be Lee's best offensive action in the war. The Union troops took a horrible beating. The Confederates paid dearly, also, for it was at this location that Stonewall Jackson was mortally wounded. General Lee stated that he had lost his "right arm" and was

Chapter 23

devastated at the loss of Jackson. The South won the battle at Chancellorsville, and the Union troops withdrew to lick their wounds.

Encouraged by the victory at Chancellorsville, General Lee planned his next move - an offensive invasion of a major northern town. He believed that if he captured a city such as Baltimore, Maryland, Lincoln would pull troops away from the Mississippi River. Lee also hoped that his hungry troops would find enough supplies and food as they made their way through the bountiful fields of Pennsylvania.

As Lee marched his army through western Maryland and into Pennsylvania, he decided to stop in the small town of Gettysburg to purchase some badly needed supplies. It was in Gettysburg that a Union scout troop saw the Confederates and scrambled to warn their officers of the Rebel army's presence.

The armies met on two ridges outside of Gettysburg. The fighting that ensued was the most terrible, and probably one of the most famous battles, in the Civil War. For three days, the armies faced each other down. At the end of the first day, Lee's troops forced the Northern army back, but did not break them. On the second day, Lee attacked from the side, but he was beaten back. The battle of the third day began with the heaviest fighting so far.

> **F.Y.I.**
>
> The Emancipation Proclamation was written in 1862. It was a savvy political move on Lincoln's part. Although Lincoln's original purpose for the war was to preserve the Union, freeing the slaves became an obvious necessity.
>
> When President Lincoln issued the Emancipation Proclamation, it was, in part, to encourage the South to give up. This proclamation seemed to breathe life into the battle-weary North. They were no longer fighting only for the preservation of the Union, but to make "all men free!" The freed slaves joined the Union army by the tens of thousands.

Chapter 23

At the end of the Battle of Gettysburg, the Union soldiers, under the newly-appointed General Meade, watched the Confederates turn and head back to Virginia, their baggage and wounded making a seventeen mile long train behind them. General Meade did not command the Union troops to follow them. At the end of the battle, President Lincoln assigned a new general, William T. Sherman, to serve in the West. General Grant was brought from guarding the Mississippi area and made the commanding officer in the Union Army. General Meade was assigned to serve under General Grant.

> **F.Y.I.** When Abraham Lincoln won the election of 1864, his new vice president was a Southerner named Andrew Johnson. Lincoln hoped that by having Johnson as the vice president, the South would come more willingly back into the Union. In this election, Lincoln's political opponent was former Union general George McClellan.

Sherman and Grant worked methodically together to create a vice grip on the South. Their goal was to destroy any property that might supply much-needed goods to the hungry Southerners. Sherman made a famous "March to the Sea," leaving behind mass destruction in every village, town, and city that he and his troops swept through.

General Sherman

By early to mid December, Sherman's men had reached Savannah, Georgia, a Confederate port city. Savannah fell easily to the Union soldiers, which cut off the supplies that came through her harbors. After defeating Savannah, Sherman turned his forces north.

In June 1864, Grant crossed the James River with the intention of attacking Richmond. To accomplish this, he needed to take the town of Petersburg. General Lee heard of the town's plight and came to their rescue, and Grant's troops settled in for a siege of Petersburg, which by its end, would be eighteen months long. By March 1865, Lee realized that there was no winning this battle, locked up in the city. With the 54,000 men left

Chapter 23

in his army, Lee tried to lure Grant out into the open. Grant's army outnumbered the hungry Confederate soldiers more than two to one; Lee had to fall back.

Lee decided that he would try to run west with his men to find a place to regroup and rebuild, but Sheridan blocked his retreat. On April 19, 1865, near the Appomattox Courthouse, Lee's men tried to take one last stand. When that failed, General Lee, recognizing that it was over, asked for terms of surrender. The terms were generous. No war prisoners would be kept. Soldiers could have their horses to ride home. Officers were allowed to keep their weapons. As soon as the soldiers pledged they would not take up arms again, they were given enough supplies to get them home.

As news of Lee's surrender spread to far-reaching western troops, Confederate soldiers laid down their arms to return to their loved ones. The war had taken its toll on our country. Approximately one-third of the two million men, who served in the war, were killed or injured. The South was hit the hardest, with one-fourth of all military-aged men, dead.

The war may have been over, but there was deep rooted bitterness left behind. The North had won the war to keep the South in the Union and to free the slaves, but there was mutual distrust. It would take decades to work past these problems, because each side blamed the other for the loss caused by the war.

Chapter 24 — Reconstruction

"With malice toward none; with charity for all; with firmness in the right, let us strive on to finish the work we are in; to bind up the nation's wounds; to care for him who shall have borne the battle, and for his widow, and his orphan - to do all which may achieve and cherish a just, and a lasting peace, among ourselves, and with all nations." Abraham Lincoln - second inaugural speech given just weeks before the end of the Civil War and his own untimely death.

On Good Friday, April 14, 1865, President Lincoln and his wife, Mary, attended a play at Ford's theater. An angry Confederate sympathizer slipped into the box and shot the president in the back of the head. Abraham Lincoln died the next morning. The assassin, John Wilkes Booth, was captured and killed. The nation was in shock. What would happen next? Who would lead our nation in the reconstruction process?

Following the war, the North had an easier time recovering than the South. The North had not been as devastated by the war. Their industry had continued throughout the war, and immigration had kept the population from severe depletion. In contrast, the South had not only lost their way of life; they had lost their slaves. Many Southerners had suffered severe poverty during the war, and many of the cities and towns had been almost completely destroyed. Fields had been stripped bare, railroads demolished, and businesses bankrupted. The Confederate money system was, of course, worth nothing now, and the plantation system was obsolete. Very few Southerners had money worth anything.

Another problem the South faced was the former slaves. Many of them did not have the skills to do any kind of work other than what they had done as slaves. They had been an important part of the South's economy as slaves, but as freedmen, they had no place at

Chapter 24

all in Southern society. The nation was going to have to work hard to "absorb" this people group.

Before President Lincoln died, he had given careful consideration of how he wanted the reconstruction to take place. He wanted the South to be allowed to come back into the Union with as little delay as possible. Many in Congress believed Lincoln's plan was too kind to the South. They believed the South needed to earn their way back into the Union. After Lincoln's assassination, Andrew Johnson became president. You will remember that Lincoln had chosen Johnson as a running-mate because Johnson was from the South. Andrew Johnson was the only senator from Tennessee to keep his position during the war. Johnson was outspokenly against the South's behavior, and when he became president, he wanted to make them jump through some hoops before they could re-enter the Union.

> **F.Y.I.**
>
> **A man without a country...**
> General Robert E. Lee, the major Confederate general of the Civil War, lived the remainder of his days without regaining his American citizenship. As a general in the Confederacy, he had committed treason and had lost his citizenship, but when he surrendered his request to be pardoned and reinstated as a United States citizen, his application was never processed. It was in June of 1974, one hundred ten years after Lee had lost his citizenship, that Congress finally declared him to be a citizen of America.

Johnson's requirements included each southern state pledging a loyalty oath to the Union and individual pardons for anyone with holdings of over $20,000. Another requirement was each state had to ratify the 13th amendment which made slavery illegal. Until the citizens of a state met the requirements, they were not allowed to vote or hold offices in the government.

The country's political atmosphere was extremely chaotic at the time. There were hard feelings between the Republican and Democratic parties. The various opinions of what should be done about reconstruction made it difficult for anyone to make a final decision about anything. To make matters much worse, the black people were being discriminated against

Chapter 24

and persecuted by those who were bitter about the war's outcome. Many southern states had black codes, to "help control the black population." These codes were extremely unfair; they prevented blacks from doing almost anything but menial labor. Some states' black codes forbade blacks to live inside the towns or cities of that state. Many codes told blacks what type of occupations they could or could not have. These codes were oppressive to the newly freed black people, and they did nothing to help the reconstruction of the country.

In 1867, a radical legislation was passed in Congress. The Reconstruction Act of 1867 went far beyond what either Lincoln or Andrew Johnson had wanted to require of the South. This legislation put the South under martial law, splitting it into five military districts governed by a Union general. The legislation also stated that blacks could vote and hold political offices.

Under this new legislation, if a state wanted to re-enter the Union, they had to hold public conventions where there were both black and white voting delegates. These states also were required to write new state constitutions following the outline that Congress laid out. The Reconstruction Act of 1867 also required any state seeking re-entry into the Union to ratify the fourteenth amendment, which outlined the newly defined definition of citizenship requirements.

President Johnson was extremely unpopular with the congress. His views of what the reconstruction should look like varied sharply from theirs. They passed the Radical Reconstruction Act, even though Johnson had vetoed it, but they were concerned because he held the executive power to appoint officials. Congress, worried that he would exercise this power to replace those who opposed him, passed the Tenure of Office Act in 1867. This act made it illegal for presidentially appointed officers to be removed unless the removal was approved by the Senate.

Johnson put this legislation to the test by removing Lincoln's hold over Secretary of War, Edwin Stanton. The real issue at stake was whether or not to allow the radicals to remove the president, because they did not agree with him politically. At the end, the vote was one senator short of impeaching Johnson. Andrew Johnson finished his term, and the presidency was preserved. Years afterward, the Tenure of Office was declared

Chapter 24

unconstitutional and was repealed. Johnson was cleared of any wrong-doing. Eventually, the radicals lost their control of the country's politics, and the South was able to complete their reconstruction phase on their own, in their own way.

The years following the reconstruction slowly grew into a boom time of invention and advancements. Natural resources were discovered, immigration swelled, and transportation and technology advanced. America was finally moving forward.

> **Scalawags & Carpetbaggers**
> Northerners who went to the South to help with the reconstruction efforts, were called "Carpetbaggers." Many of these folks were opportunists seeking political and/or financial gain. Just like in every group of people, there were those with good intentions and those with greedy motives.
> "Scalawags" were white Southerners who supported the Radical Reconstruction legislation.

F.Y.I.

Chapter 25 — The Big Business Boom

In the years surrounding the Civil War, the government was eager to have more railroads in the nation. To aid in the development of the railroad companies, they made policies that not only provided financial aid, but also provided the land on which to build the railroads. The goal was to construct a railroad that stretched across the nation - a transcontinental railroad.

In 1864, the government charted two railroad companies, the Union Pacific and the Central Pacific, to work on the Transcontinental Railroad. The Union Pacific worked westward, using Irish workers and later, Civil War veterans. The Central Pacific worked eastward using mostly Chinese workers. The two companies raced toward each other, each trying to reach the meeting point, Promontory Point, Utah. In 1862 and 1864, the government gave the railroad companies a four hundred foot wide strip of land through the territories in which rails were being laid.

By 1885, railroads were linking Lake Superior and the Pacific Ocean. Duluth, Minnesota, had a line to Portland, as well as Oregon, Spokane, and Tacoma, Washington. James J. Hill, a millionaire from St. Paul, Minnesota, privately funded the Great Northern Railroad, another transcontinental line, with branches up into Canada.

Let's take a moment to look at a few of the big businessmen who helped America grow during this time...

Cornelius Vanderbilt was one of these big businessmen. Vanderbilt started his career as a ferryman when he was sixteen years old and grew his business by buying out his steamboat competitors. He put his plan into action by forcing his competitors into selling him all of their railroad lines. Little by little, Vanderbilt grew his business by

Cornelius Vanderbilt

149

Chapter 25

John D. Rockefeller

buying out his steamboat competitors and taking over the management of the railroads, which connected to his steamboat routes. In 1847, Mr. Vanderbilt took over the presidency of the Stonington Railroad Company. Eventually, Vanderbilt became an extremely wealthy man by controlling most of the railroads in the country.

John D. Rockefeller, another of America's major businessmen of this time period, was an oilman. Rockefeller and his associates formed the first trust by combining several companies to make a huge corporation, Standard Oil. By the 1880s, other industries were following Rockefeller's example.

Andrew Carnegie

Andrew Carnegie was a steel tycoon. He built his empire with the help and expertise of multiple business partners. It is Carnegie who is responsible for the Eads Bridge in St. Louis, Missouri. This spectacular bridge is made out of steel and is the first bridge to span the Mississippi River.

Technology advanced quickly during these post-reconstruction years. Alexander Graham Bell's invention of the telephone set the whole world on its ear. Major inventions like this had the capability of opening up whole new industries as well as changing the average American's life. During the 1880s and 1890s, the number of patents issued through the patent office averaged more than twenty thousand per year.

Electricity became more understood and appreciated during this time period, which was quickly becoming known as the Industrial Revolution. Electricity helped scientists make *huge* leaps in inventions. Thomas Edison showed the country that electricity could be helpful in everyday life. His lightbulb lit excitement all across America. Edison also showed the world

Chapter 25

exciting inventions, such as the first moving picture camera. Industrialism had changed the face of America in just a couple, short decades.

Not all the changes in our country were good, however. Sometimes in their climb to get to the top, economic opportunists were completely satisfied to step on the workers below them. Unfair working conditions and low wages were common. In some cases, company owners became extremely wealthy, while their laborers toiled for long, hard hours, doing dangerous and difficult work.

It was during this period that a theory came to light that helped support this way of thinking. A man named Charles Darwin was searching for answers, just like every human being does, but instead of finding the true answers to his questions, Darwin spent five years concocting a completely erroneous theory, which completely removed God from the picture. This theory states, among other things, that only the strongest of each species survives. This crazy notion made people believe that it's acceptable to treat other people poorly and unfairly; if they don't survive, they aren't strong. Unfortunately, the theory of evolution is still widely embraced in the scientific world.

Not everyone was buying into the "survival of the strongest" theory, though. Up to this point, the American government had not interfered with the industrial world. In 1887, the Interstate Commerce Act was a reaction to the ruthless practices of the railroads. Prior to this act, individual states were responsible for regulation the railroads. But because some states had little interest in protecting or interfering, the railroaders got away with much more in those states.

Over the next few years, the country started to move toward more regulations, stating what types of business and industry practices were illegal. These legislations were not perfect and some were hardly effective at all, but it was an important step in the right direction.

The Sherman Anti-trust Act of 1890 declared that trusts restrained trade, and that this restraint "was illegal." Because the act didn't define "restraint of trade," big businesses

Chapter 25

worked their way around the restrictions. Most of the time the courts ruled in favor of the big businesses.

The government was not the only one concerned about the future of American industry. The factory workers, who suffered injustice and unfair working conditions on a daily basis, began to protest. Sometimes these protests were "unofficial" as groups of workers came together in order to find a solution to their problems. Other times, the protests were well-organized groups called unions. These unions not only worked for better conditions in the workplace, but also for better living conditions and benefits for veterans and immigrants.

One of the biggest union groups was the Knights of Labor, which had its beginnings back in 1869. The Knights of Labor sought better pay for all workers. They also worked for better working conditions and more humane hours. By 1886, the Knights of Labor had 700,000 members.

The American Federation of Labor was another major labor union, started in 1881. This union was different from the Knights of Labor in several ways. The most important reason was the American Federation of Labor only allowed skilled workers to join the Union. Workers joined local divisions of the union. These local divisions, or "craft unions," worked with workers of the same trade.

Chapter 26 — The Turn of the Century

Note: Before you read this chapter, please complete the Day 1 assignment in your Student's Journal.

The nineteenth century saw America increase in population, struggle to free itself from slavery, and move into a fantastic age of invention. As we learned in our last chapter, the country didn't grow without experiencing growing pains. Labor unions and legislation, handed down from the government, sought to level the playing field. Some of these efforts paid off, and some of them didn't, but at least society as a whole was moving toward awareness.

By the close of the 1800s, America was beginning to be recognized as an impressive world power, although America herself was far more interested in her own business than what was going on in the world as a whole. Most people lived like they should mind their own business and stay out of the world's politics.

It was around the turn of the century that some American politicians started to observe how European super-powers were building their power by gaining control in foreign lands. Many of these European nations were colonizing areas of these lands, thus spreading their empires much further than their own immediate countrysides. These were called imperialist countries. Some Americans believed that United States should follow suit and become an imperialist nation, also. In their minds, there were many reasons to move the United States in that direction.

Military gain was thought to be one of the most important reasons. By gaining territories in other nations, the military would build extensive military bases and properties in many areas around the world. Of course, only slightly less important to the imperialists was the desire to build wealth. Having colonies in other lands would open trade and opportunity for businessmen to hire local workers at low wages, therefore making higher profits.

Chapter 26

Not all desire for colonization was fueled by the desire to gain wealth. Some Americans desired to colonize, because they realized that there were many people groups living in extreme poverty. Outreach to these groups would be much more effective if there were American establishments in those lands. The Gospel could also be preached to these people. These types of efforts are called humanitarianism, and in the 1880s, the idea of spreading hope and help began to spread, gaining more and more attention and popularity.

One man who was instrumental in this missionary movement was Dwight L. Moody. This evangelist, with a missionary's heart, moved hundreds of young Americans and British to join him in his missionary efforts.

The United States bought a piece of "distant land" in 1867. Alaska, which is not connected to the rest of the country, belonged to Russia. Gold was soon discovered along the Yukon River, and soon thousands of miners rushed to the area. The gold discovery boosted the whole country's economy. Alaska did not become a state until 1959, but the natural resources, including silver, copper, and a huge amount of oil, have proven extremely beneficial to the nation as a whole.

The United States also annexed Hawaii in 1898. American businessmen had taken over the economy in Hawaii by building huge plantations, run by poor locals, who were paid pitifully low wages. In 1893, they forced the Hawaiian queen, Liliuokalani (lee-LEE-oo-oh-kah-LAH-nee), from power. President Cleveland refused to annex Hawaii, because of the way the queen had been removed, but President McKinley agreed in 1898.

Around the turn of the Century, the population of the United States was seventy-five million and growing. With the giant growth of the population came the need to build better housing, make cleaner neighborhoods, and provide better education. By the year 1900, urbanization, the mass-movement into the cities, was bogging down the improvement efforts.

The massive apartment complexes designed and built, with the intentions of improving air quality and making safer, cleaner housing for the newly-arriving immigrants, failed miserably. Between the years of 1900 and 1910, 8.8 million immigrants came to America. The majority of this great flood of people ended up in the horrible tenement houses, crammed tightly together. Sanitation was poor, and crime was high. Despite all of the hard living conditions, these immigrants were determined to make a good life for their family and future generations. Schools, at that time, did not offer bilingual classes, which forced the immigrant children to learn English quickly. In turn, the children taught their parents the new language.

Education became much more available during this time. In the year 1860, the United States had only three hundred secondary public schools. Most of the schools available were elementary level. By the year 1900, there were 6,000 public secondary schools, and by 1915, 12,000 had been established. Higher education was much more readily available to people from a wider spectrum of life.

These were the Americans who contributed so greatly to the building of the country. They were not only laborers in all the varying American industries, but they also brought with them their distinct traditions and customs from their homelands. It was in this way that America became the great "melting pot of the world." These immigrants made up most of the American lower class. But many did not stay there! As the economy improved, many Americans had more free time, thanks to the convenience brought by inventions.

This free time was spent in more entertaining ways than any other time in the history of our nation up to this point. Baseball games became extremely popular; the first World Series took place in the year 1903. Rollerskating, boxing, basketball, football, and heavy weight fighting competitions were all popular pastimes.

Education and opportunity was changing the face of America's culture. For the first time, there was a middle class. It was this class that drove the country's economy. The middle class, although not considered wealthy, had enough money to purchase the mass-produced items that made life more comfortable. Many families in the middle class had worked hard and now could afford comfortable homes, furnished in the latest designs.

This was the Victorian Age, and the style was to have rich-looking and rather elaborate furnishings in your home. Heavy brocade curtains and flowery printed floor

Chapter 26

coverings graced many American sitting rooms. Beautiful light fixtures and heavy wooden door and window trim made homes look and feel lavish.

There were still those, however, that remained painfully aware of the less fortunate in our country. Child labor laws were called for, and many reformers began demanding Washington D.C.'s attention. This era would become known as the Progressive Era. People wanted change, and many believed that it was the government's duty to make it happen.

Temperance groups were calling for the government to shut down any establishment that they deemed corruptive to American culture as a whole. These groups wanted the government to make gambling, drinking alcohol, and some types of dancing illegal. The Progressives demanded change.

The Founding Fathers could not make allowances for every future situation our country would face; they had no way of knowing what the future held. Because of this, each decade's and century's public servants and elected officials have had the responsibility to interpret the Constitution in the light of their current issues.

Do you think the Progressives were right? What do you think the government's role is (if any) in reforming the culture?

The presidents of the early 1900s were of the progressive mindset. Theodore Roosevelt, our 26th president, was the first progressive president. (You learned about Theodore Roosevelt when you researched the Spanish/American War.) President Theodore Roosevelt was extremely popular. Roosevelt believed that workers should have fair wages, better working hours, and more comfortable working conditions. He claimed that he wanted to give both management and labor a "square deal."

> **F.Y.I.** Upton Sinclair's *The Jungle* exposed the horrors of the meat packing industry before the Pure Food and Drug Act was passed.

In 1906, Congress passed the Pure Food and Drug Act. This act gave governmental inspectors the responsibility and the right to inspect all slaughterhouses and meat packing factories. The act clamped down on patent medicines, also. These medicines, available by

Chapter 26

Theodore Roosevelt

mail order or at many drugstores, were mostly alcohol and an opium byproduct. Besides being expensive and therefore a lucrative business for the "medicine company," these drugs were highly addictive and exceedingly harmful. The Pure Food and Drug Act demanded that all products had to have a list of their ingredients on the label.

Theodore Roosevelt also felt strongly that our nation desperately needed to reserve and protect more areas of land for the future generations of Americans. Between 1901 and 1906, the following national parks were established: Wind Cave (1901), Crater Lake (1902), Mesa Verde (1906), the Petrified Forest (1906), and Platt (1906). In establishing these national parks, President Roosevelt more than doubled the acreage in reserve.

President William H. Taft followed Roosevelt in office and was also a progressive president and was successful in office. Taft backed reform in the post office, created the Department of Labor to protect the workers of America, organized the Children's Bureau to end child labor, and saw the Sixteenth and Seventeenth Amendments to the Constitution ratified. Although he had accomplished a large amount during his term, Taft did not have the magnetic personality of Roosevelt; therefore, he was not as popular with the American people.

Both Roosevelt and Taft were Republicans, but the next president, Woodrow Wilson, was a Democrat - and a Progressive. Instead of trying to regulate large companies with governmental restrictions, Wilson thought the best way to deal with them was to break them up. In his thinking, small companies couldn't form monopolies (when a large company almost completely

William Taft

Chapter 26

Woodrow Wilson

controls a certain industry).

President Wilson took two steps to gain control of the big businesses. First, he set up the Federal Trade Commission. Next, he asked Congress to pass the Clayton Anti-trust Act in 1914. These acts were heavily weighted in favor of unions and farmers' cooperatives, giving them power to legally protest what they considered unfair treatment. Wilson is also responsible for establishing the Federal Reserve System.

The Electoral College

Chapter 27: The Election Process Part 1

Chapter 28: The Election Process Part 2

Please Leave Blank.

The Election Process
Part 1

Does our voting and election system seem like a mystery to you? You have probably watched your parents vote for their choice of elected officials. Have you ever wondered how their ballots were counted, and if their candidate was elected, could it have been their vote that mattered? Maybe you have wondered if it even matters if you vote or not. Does it really depend on the peoples' votes, or is the election decided beforehand?

The answers to these questions are important to understand. Although individual votes do matter, a presidential election is not decided by the popular vote. Do you remember when we learned about the difference between a direct democracy and a representative democracy? The direct democracy is run directly by the people, and a representative democracy is run by representatives that groups of people vote for to represent them in the government. In some ways, our election system is set up like this also. Let's take a look at how the Electoral College has evolved over the years.

Our country uses a system called the Electoral College. Article 2 of the Constitution states that the president is chosen by electors. These electors are similar to the representatives. When a citizen goes into a voting booth, closes the curtain, and carefully fills in the circle next to their candidates of choice, they are not directly voting for the person they want to be the president and vice president of the country, they are actually voting for a slate or list of electors, who have promised to vote for that certain candidate in the electoral college.

But what is this Electoral College? Who designed it? What is the reason for it? Has the Electoral College changed over the years? How does it work today? These are questions we will explore together over the next two chapters. First, we will discover how the Electoral College came to be. I think you will find that it was borne from necessity. Remember, our country's government was an experiment - a grand and wonderful experiment!

Chapter 27

In the summer of 1787, the Founding Fathers met to design our new government. We have learned that they worked together, debating, arguing, and praying, until they could come up with a compromise on almost every element of the Constitution. As they talked about how the president should be elected, there were many various ideas and opinions. Some thought that the president and vice president should be chosen by Congress. The argument against this idea was the president might feel obligated to Congress and be inclined to agree with them more readily. Likewise, they felt that if the state legislatures chose the president, he would feel obligated to those particular states.

The delegates discussed designing an election by popular vote, where the people actually voted for their favored candidate, but they feared that the people from each state would only vote for candidates from their own state. This could cause quite a mess. Because of the poor conditions of roads, political campaigning would be nearly impossible. The delegates continued to work on their ideas until they came up with a compromise they could all agree upon. This compromise states that a college or group of electors would be established to elect the President. Electors, the Founding Fathers stated emphatically, needed to be men of character; learned men, who were knowledgeable in the runnings of our country's government.

The Constitution set these requirements for the Electoral College:

1. Each state was entitled to the same number of electors as it had representatives and senators in Congress.
2. Congress left it up to the state legislatures as to how their electors would be chosen.
3. No elected officials, such as senators and representatives, or any federal employee would be allowed to serve as an elector.
4. Each state's electors would meet in their own state in order to keep from influencing each other, rather than in one central location.
5. The electors had to vote for two candidates, one of whom had to be from a state other than their own.
6. The finished votes had to be sealed and sent to the president of the Senate,

then opened and read to the Congress.

7. The candidate who received more than half of the votes (over half of the total) would become the president. Whoever received the next greatest number of votes became the vice president.

8. If none of the candidates had an absolute majority, the House of Representatives would decide who had won from the top five candidates. If there was a tie for the vice presidency, the Senate would choose the winner.

In 1788, during the presidential election, only ten of the thirteen states participated in the process. New York legislature missed the deadline because they couldn't agree on electors. North Carolina and Rhode Island had not ratified their constitutions and were not officially part of the Union yet. It was a rather mixed bag of methods in that first election.

The 1796 Election

John Adams ran as a Federalist. He favored a stronger central government and a national bank system. Adams was popular with the bigger businessmen of New England. John Adams won the presidential vote with 71 electoral votes.

Thomas Jefferson led the Democratic-Republican party. He stood for smaller central government and more state control. Jefferson was popular with the farmers. Even though he held vastly different political views than Adams, Jefferson was named vice-president, because he had come in second.

Chapter 27

This election as well as the election of 1800, showed a major flaw in the election system. We learned how Adams ran again with Charles C. Pinckney as his vice-president, while Jefferson ran with Aaron Burr. The mess that came from the electoral counts resulted in heated debates in the House. Everyone agreed on one point: something needed to change - the Constitution would need to be amended and the process to elect the vice-president changed. The Twelfth Amendment was decided and ratified quickly, and everyone hoped that the problem was solved.

The Twelfth Amendment said:

- The electors would cast one vote for the presidential candidate and another for the vice-presidential candidate.

- The presidential candidate with the most votes won.

- The House would choose from the top three candidates, in the case of no one having the majority.

- The vice presidential candidate with the majority would win the office. If no one had the majority, the Senate would choose a winner from the top two.

- Each state would continue to have one vote.

The process still required a fair amount of fine tuning, however. In the 1824 election, there were six candidates running for the office of president. Andrew Jackson, John Quincy Adams, William Crawford, and Henry Clay were all from the Democratic-Republican party, although they all held varying political views. Andrew Jackson won the most electoral votes, but he did not win the majority. As was outlined in the Constitution, the House of Representatives chose the president. They chose John Quincy Adams; Andrew Jackson was the first president to have the highest popular vote but fail to be elected.

By the mid-1800s, the political world was dominated by two major political parties - the Democrats and the Republicans. The years following the Civil War were marked by political wars between the Radical Republicans, who stripped the voting rights from the Southern whites while giving them to the former slaves. Eventually, the Southern whites retaliated by overthrowing the Radical's control, and by using intimidation and fraud, kept the blacks from voting.

The election of 1876 proved to be another problematic event. The Republican candidate, Rutherford B. Hayes, ran against Democrat Samuel J. Tilden. The candidates needed 185 electoral votes to have the majority. The morning after the election, it appeared that Tilden had won, even though not all of the results were in. What ensued was a battle between the Republican electors and the Democratic electors. Congress finally appointed an electoral commission to decide which set of electoral votes would decide the election. This commission was an exercise in non-partisan fairness: five members from the Senate, five from the House, and five from the Supreme Court. Eventually, a balance of Republican and Democratic congressmen, senators, and judges were chosen, and the vote was cast. The results showed eight to seven in Haye's favor.

After the 1876 election, Congress passed the Electoral Count Act of 1887. This act stated that it was the individual states' responsibility to resolve their own electoral disputes. Each state had the final say in deciding between competing slates of electors. The designated officer in each state could validate its choice of electors, but Congress was still allowed to dispute the electoral vote. This act was tested in the following year's presidential election. Benjamin Harrison won the majority in the Electoral College even though Grover Cleveland won the popular vote, but unlike the election of 1876, conflict was resolved much more smoothly.

Chapter 28  The Election Process
Part 2

In our last chapter, we discussed how the election process started, some of the problems it posed for our country, and how we moved toward a more streamlined Electoral College. In the deeper research in your journal, you will see that we still do not have a perfect Electoral College, and what we do now if there is an issue in the election process.

So how are electors chosen? In most states, political parties are responsible for choosing their own state's slate of electors. Sometimes these electors are chosen because of their service to that political party. If a party's candidate wins that state's popular vote, the party's electors participate in the Electoral College and cast their votes at a meeting in December.

Every state has the same number of electors as it does senators and representatives in Congress. Every state has two senators, but the number of representatives depends on the state's population. Some of the states have many more representatives than the others because of their large populations. For example, Florida has 25 representatives and 2 senators, therefore, they have 27 electors, while the state of Montana has only 1 representative and 2 senators, giving them 3 electors. Although Washington D.C. is not technically a state, it has participated in the elector college since 1961, when the Twenty-third Amendment gave them the same number of electors as the smallest state.

A state's population can become larger or smaller, which affects the number of their representatives, in turn affecting their number of electors. The state's population is determined by a census every ten years. At the time of writing this book (early 2014), there are 435 Representatives in the House, and as always, 100 Senators, which means that there are 538 electors (with the additional 3 from Washington D.C.). For a presidential candidate to have the majority, they must have more than 270 of the electoral votes. Electors in all fifty states are chosen on the Tuesday after the first Monday in November. The governor of each of the states submits a Certificate of Ascertainment to the Archivist of the United States. The document lists the slate of electors and how many votes were received.

Chapter 28

To help us understand the process a little better, let's read this quote from historian, David Barton:

"The popular vote in each State directs the electors of that State how to cast their vote for President. In most States, whichever candidate wins the popular vote in that State wins all of that State's electors; but since the manner of choosing a State's electors is left by the Constitution to each State, different States, not surprisingly, have different rules. For example, in Maine and Nebraska, the winner does not take all; rather, the candidate who wins the popular vote in each congressional district wins the electoral vote from that congressional district, and the candidate who wins the entire State receives the State's two remaining electoral votes.

The presidential electors are usually selected in each State at the same time that each political party in that State determines its presidential candidate. That is, when a State party selects its presidential nominee it also designates a slate of electors. These electors, along with the party's nominees for president and vice-president, are submitted to the chief election official in the State. Thus, in each State there is a slate of Republican electors, Democrat electors, Green Party electors, Reform Party electors, etc., and the candidate that wins the popular vote in that State will have the electors from his or her own political party cast the electoral votes for that State. As constitutional scholar William Rawle explained in his classic 1825 commentaries on the Constitution:

```
'[T]he electors do not assemble in their several States for a free exercise
of their own judgments, but for the purpose of electing the particular
candidate who happens to be preferred by the predominant political party
which has chosen those electors.' [William Rawle, A View of the Constitution
of the United States of America (Philadelphia: Philip H. Nicklin, 1829), p.
57.]
```

If a presidential candidate receives an absolute majority of electoral votes, that candidate becomes the President and will be sworn into office on noon, January 20th. If no candidate receives an absolute majority, as happened in the 1824 election when the electoral votes were split among four candidates, or if there should be a tie (if, for example, two candidates each received 269 votes), then the House of Representatives chooses the President from among the top three contenders, with each State being allotted only one vote on behalf of its State, regardless of the size of its congressional delegation. The Senate chooses the Vice-President in a similar manner."(1)

Chapter 28

The Electoral College has been attacked as unconstitutional, with opponents calling for an amendment to abolish it. Many believe that it is not a true "for the people, by the people" method of choosing our president and vice-president. What do you think? Would you agree with them, or do you think the Electoral College keeps our elections from turning into mass chaos?

America, a World Power

1900 - 1990

Chapter 29: America and the Great War

Chapter 30: The Roaring Twenties & The Dirty Thirties

Chapter 31: America in World War 2

Chapter 32: America in the Last 50 Years

Please Leave Blank.

Chapter 29  America and the Great War

Between the years 1914 through 1916, America watched as Europe engaged in an absolutely horrific war. On June 29, 1914, the newspapers reported the assassination of Archduke Francis Ferdinand, the heir to the Austro-Hungarian throne. Most Americans probably did not realize this assassination on the other side of the world would affect their lives in drastic ways. The world was about to erupt into a war. Major alliances of nations, pledging each other military support, were drawing lines in the dust.

The Triple Alliance included Germany, Austria-Hungary, and Italy. All three of these countries were united by their imperialistic goals. The Triple Entente (on-TONT) included Britain, France, and Russia - joined mostly by their fear of Germany. Each of these alliances involved major European powers, which made it much more likely that other countries around the world would be drawn into the fighting. The United States was not involved in European alliances or disagreements, and so it simply watched as peace began to unravel and fighting erupted.

Germany made the first move by tromping destructively through neutral Belgium to northern France. British troops came to the aid of France before Germany could take over the country, and both sides settled into trench warfare stretching from the English Channel to the Rhine River. While this was going on, the Russian army began a series of unsuccessful attacks against Germany and Austria-Hungary from the east.

Both sides introduced new weapons and equipment, which brought an element of brutality into the war that had never been experienced before. The British developed the tank, which enabled them to drive through a heavy barrage of firing. The tank made it possible for advancement even through extremely rough terrain, while firing a continual round of shells. It wasn't long before the other nations developed their own tanks.

In April of 1915, Germany unleashed a new, secret weapon - poison gas. This terrifying weapon damaged the nose, throat, and lungs of anyone who breathed it in.

Chapter 29

Mustard gas, as it was called, became even more feared than the tanks. The gas mask was soon developed and became a part of every soldier's equipment on the battle field. Many civilians living in the war-torn areas of Europe also wore gas masks; even animals had their own style of these protective masks.

Fighting was also happening in the air. Germany used zeppelins, aircrafts similar to blimps, to drop bombs on Britain. These large aircrafts were extremely slow, making them hard to steer and maneuver. Soon airplanes replaced the zeppelins, and the war took on a whole new aspect; never before had air raids been a part of wars. These new air war machines were used for aerial reconnaissance, bombing, and what was called "dogfighting."

Before 1915, pilots could not fire their aircraft guns forward without shooting their own propellors. Dogfighting between aircrafts became possible when the guns were synchronized with the propellors. F.Y.I.

Fighter pilots gained celebrity status when they shot down more than five enemy planes. These flying aces, as they came to be called, were heroes of the war, and each country had their own. The German flying ace, Manfred von Richthofen, became "the Red Baron," while Britain's flying ace was Mick Mannock. (When the United States became involved with the war, the most famous American ace was Eddie Rickenbacker.)

The Great War was the first war with battles on ground, in the air, in the water, and under the water. The Germans perfected the submarine and used these underwater boats (called U-boats) to send torpedos into the sides of unsuspecting enemy ships. This war was also marked by the improvement in transportation, as trucks and automobiles helped with the transportation of military personnel and supplies.

Although America was not officially part of the action in the war, it was not completely unaffected by it. President Wilson stated that all Americans should remain neutral in action and in word, but as the war in Europe progressed, this became more and more difficult for several reasons. First, most American favored the Allied (Britain, France, and Russia) and their cause. Although there were millions of Americans who had roots in Germany, many more were descended from British ancestry. The American legal system, part of its form of government, and its language were all from an English background. France, too, was favored over Germany, because of the help they had given America throughout the years. Germany had become an object of scorn when they had ruthlessly marched through neutral Belgium; invading a neutral country did not set well with many nations around the world.

The second reason for the Americans favoring the Allied cause was economic. Since Britain and France were major trade partners, Americans felt more on their side. Because of this favoritism, America gradually began aiding the Allies by selling great shipments of products needed to fight the war. When the Allies ran low on money, America loaned them what they needed to continue. Of course, this infuriated the Central Powers (Germany, Austria-Hungary, and Italy), because it was American-made bullets that were killing their soldiers. President Wilson did not stop these business deals, however.

Germany's hateful behavior did nothing to win the Americans' approval, and the British and French made sure the United States heard all about what was going on in the war. When Germans executed five thousand Belgian citizens for resisting, the news quickly traveled over the British and French controlled trans-Atlantic cables to the American newspaper offices. It was becoming more and more difficult for America to stay out of the war, and when a German U-boat sank a British sea liner, the *Lusitania*, killing 1,198 passengers - including 128 Americans, President Wilson demanded an apology and threatened to withdraw diplomatic recognition. Germany decided to play it safer for a while, but when they announced that they would assume "unrestricted submarine warfare," President Wilson cut off all diplomatic relations with them.

In March 1917, British intelligence intercepted a telegram between Germany and the minister of Mexico. Germany was offering Mexico a reward - the return of Texas, New Mexico, and Arizona - for entering the war against the United States if we chose to enter the war. President Wilson requested that Congress arm American merchant ships and released the intercepted telegram to the American public. Americans were irate, and that anger grew when three more American merchant ships were sunk. On April 2, 1917, President Wilson gravely appeared before both houses of Congress to request a declaration of war. On April 6th, the United States joined the war.

When the United States entered the war, the country scrambled to get ready. There were not enough standing soldiers, and the equipment was sorely lacking. America had no tanks and only enough ammunition for a nine or ten hour long bombardment. Men had to be trained, equipment manufactured, supplies gathered, and ships built to take the whole lot of them over to Europe.

For the first time since the Civil War, a draft was executed, and as men poured into recruitment offices across the nation, they were processed and immediately sent to one of the thirty-two training camps all across the nation. The whole country shifted to adjust to the war. As men left, the government had to organize and begin programs to help organize the war effort. The War Industries Board organized the production needed for the war. Factories were required to be transformed to produce the needed war materials. Thousands of uniforms, guns, ammunition, medical supplies, and vehicles were all mass produced as the board set the criteria to standardize the items being manufactured.

The United States Railroad Administration took control of all railroads, in order to insure that they were being operated efficiently, as they carried the extra freight and passengers. The Fuel Administration worked to conserve and direct the use of the nation's fuel. Everyone was placed on war-time restrictions, even setting aside days that everyone walked instead of drove. These gasless days helped keep the gas usage in check.

Herbert Hoover, who had already organized a massive food relief program for Belgium, led the Food Administration. Americans were asked to set up their menus to help with the food conservation efforts. Mondays were wheatless, Tuesdays were meatless, and Thursdays were porkless. American citizens raised their own vegetables in gardens in their own backyards, and soon these vegetable patches were called "Victory Gardens," because they made more food available for the soldiers.

Chapter 29

As men fought in Europe, the work force was depleted. Many women went to work outside of the home for the first time in American history. Other women, as well as men who could not fight oversees, met in groups to help the American Red Cross by knitting sweaters and socks or rolling bandages for the soldiers. All across America, there was a tremendous war effort. Journalist, George Creel, led 150,000 people in a gigantic "advertise America" propaganda campaign. Artists designed posters and ads, and an army of lecturers delivered short speeches to local assemblies.

In Europe, the American soldiers were commanded by General John Pershing. General Pershing worked under French Supreme Allied Commander, Marshal Ferdinand Foch. By this point in the war, the French and British were discouraged and weary from the fighting. They desperately needed to be infused with a new wave of fresh soldiers. The American soldiers, who first arrived in Europe in the fall of 1917, were welcomed heartily. The "Yanks," as they were called, were basically replacing the Russians in the war.

The Germans had accomplished their goal of removing the Russians from the war by aiding the return of Vladimir Lenin. The Russians had overthrown their czar, but by this time, they were so weary from the war that they followed Lenin in the Communist Revolution. Lenin called his troops home and ended Russia's alliance with the Allied cause.

The Americans were given the mission of stopping the German advances into France. The Central Powers, led by Germany, launched an all-out offensive on the western front with the hopes of sweeping through France, taking Paris, and reaching the English Channel. By June, 1918, they were at the Marne River, about fifty miles from the French capital. A combined force of American and French soldiers fought the attacking forces, and slowly but surely, they pushed them back. By July, Paris was out of danger. The German advances were starting to fall apart, and on August 8, they suffered heavy losses at Amiens.

The war was not over, though. General Pershing obtained permission to position the U.S. Army as a separate part of a larger counter-offensive action at a place called St. Mihiel (sahn mee-YELL). More than half a million American soldiers were there. Fifteen hundred planes were ready for take off, as thirty-two hundred American and French guns barraged the Germans.

Chapter 29

The breaking point came some weeks later at the Battle of the Argonne Forest. By August 8th, the Allied troops broke through the German line, regaining France as they advanced. By the end of September, the German commander, General Paul Von Hindenburg, knew that it was over.

On November 11, 1918, the fighting stopped, and Germany signed an armistice - this day became Armistice Day, an American national holiday, which would later become Veterans Day. The Great War had taken over eight million lives and left almost twenty million wounded. In the year and a half of involvement, the United States had lost one hundred fifteen thousand men, and over two hundred thousand came home wounded.

Chapter 30 — The Roaring Twenties & the Dirty Thirties

The years directly following the Great War were full of change for the United States. Many Americans were eager to have nothing to do with world affairs and yearned to return to the isolation that had marked the country in the pre-war years. Instead, the 1920s were marked by huge changes in our culture, in our economy, and even in our clothing fashion.

Following the war, the United States' economy had to readjust to the supply and demand of normal, non-war time. The huge demand for war products had kept the country's industries and farms extremely busy, but with the end of the war, the demand for these products ended. Everything had to shift back to normal production, which meant refitting factories to make items for everyday life. During the war, farms had sent millions of tons of food for war-torn Europe; now Europe could start feeding itself again. Suddenly, there was no market for the huge surplus of food.

Soldiers returning home from war had a hard time finding jobs. While they were gone, their jobs had been filled by new immigrants and African Americans, who had moved north to fill those positions. An unfortunate result of this shift in the workforce was a lot of very angry, white American men, now out of jobs. The Ku Klux Klan saw an insurgence of new members during this time period, and violence toward minority groups - especially the African Americans. Also, during this time, new immigration laws were passed to try to control the number of immigrants who could enter the United States.

Although the economy straightened itself out for the most part, and unemployment eased itself back down to normal, many of America's farmers continued to struggle throughout the 1920s, as production and prices warred against each other. Presidents Harding and Coolidge believed that the federal government should not regulate the farming economy. Instead, they felt that the economy would regulate itself and eventually even out.

The 1920s were also marked by a strong, worldwide fear of communism. Americans had heard about how the Communists had taken over Russia. They heard the reports of the massacres, and a fear of communism began to grow - especially when they heard that the Communists intended to spread their rule anywhere they could. By 1919, the Communists had two political parties in the United States. Their goal was to cause a struggle between the common worker and the property owners. Communist-phobic Americans saw any discontentment as part of the Communist plot. A wave of terrorists, bombing threats directed at big businessmen, terrified the public. (This time period is sometimes called the "Red Scare.") Eventually, the scare died down, but not until government agents raided offices of radical organizations, and arresting and deporting 249 aliens, some of whom were Communists.

As time progressed, inventions and improvements began to greatly change the lives of the average American of the 1920s. Automobiles were more common and much more affordable. The higher volume of cars brought changes to the road systems, and more paved roads began spreading out all over the nation. Travel brought changes to business as they sprang up near major road systems, and motels, gasoline stations, and family restaurants popped up almost overnight.

Although airplanes were still not a major form of transportation, Americans were enthralled as airplane pilots won admiration for their daring, long distance flights. In 1927, a Minnesotan named Charles A. Lindbergh flew his plane, the Spirit of St. Louis, across the Atlantic Ocean, from New York to Paris in thirty-three and one half hours. Lindbergh became an instant hero.

Electricity was also becoming more common and more widely used all across the nation. It became common for families to own electric appliances, which made their lives much easier. Toasters, irons, and radios all became extremely popular time-saving devices. The family radio became especially popular, as radio stations broadcasted dramatized shows and news casts. America's economy was booming. After the initial lag after the war, the economy took off with amazing speed. Assembly lines turned out cars, one every twenty-seven seconds!

The 1920s brought a huge influx of somewhat crazy fads, also. Clothing styles changed so drastically from the decade before that many older Americans looked on in

Chapter 30

disbelief at the styles worn by many younger people. Marathon dancing, bobbed hair, and short fringed skirts were all extremely popular with many young women of the time. These young ladies, called "flappers," completely abandoned the conduct codes of their mothers and grandmothers, and instead, they smoked, drank, and wore extremely heavy eye makeup.

Gambling on horse racing, boxing, and even professional sports became extremely popular. The "Roaring Twenties" are marked by sensationalism. It seemed that the more sensational the story, the more people wanted to know about it. There were almost constant tales of how policemen had made raids on secret drinking and gambling establishments.

The Eighteenth Amendment had outlawed the making, selling, or drinking of alcohol, but that did not keep it from happening. The prohibition had been established in 1919, but illegal taverns, called "speakeasies," ran secretly in the backs of stores or warehouses. "Bootleggers" made alcohol and sold it illegally to keep these drinking establishments in business. A lot of violence surrounded the bootlegging business. Gangs, run by extremely dangerous gang bosses, ran these bootlegging rings. Al Capone led a large crime ring in Chicago. He and his gang made tens of millions of dollars in the sale of the illegal booze every year in the mid to late 1920s. Opposing gangs battled over territories, using machine guns bought on the black market.

Prohibition has been called the "noble experiment." It was an experiment to test if the government could control the moral temperature of our country. Laws making certain behavior illegal are important, but if the society as a whole does not embrace change on a personal level, government cannot do it for them. Many believe that the 1920s was a time of uncontrolled capitalism and greed, a time of immoral behavior and no guilt. What do you think? Do you think that any particular decade has marked moral decline more than others?

Chapter 30

Do you think our culture is less godly or morally driven than cultures thousands of years ago? Why or why not?

By the late 1920s, the economy seemed like it would continue to climb, with seemingly no end in sight. In 1928, Herbert Hoover declared, in his election campaign, that Americans had moved closer to triumphing over poverty than any other time in our history. Not everything was as it seemed, however, and in September of 1929, investors were beginning to grow very cautious.

"The stock market peaked on September 3, 1929 with a record close of 381.17. Trading volume was 444k shares. By the end of the same month, the market had fallen by 10% to 343. On Monday, October 29, on 16.4% shares traded, the markets fell 11.5%. By that time, the markets closed at 230.17 down 40% from its all time high. In that single day, investors lost 14 billion dollars and by the end of 1929, 40 billion dollars was lost. This crash put a lot of pressure on banks and caused a great deal of money to be taken out of the economy." (1)

The sale of stocks was sliding downward, and in October orders to sell outnumbered orders to buy. On Thursday, October 24th, investors lost nine million dollars. Many investors lost everything they had, and some could not handle the loss; there was a high number of suicides that year. The stock market crash of 1929 signaled the beginning of the Great Depression. The decade that followed was marked by severe drought, widespread famine, and an extreme crash of the American economy and culture.

The 1930s, the Dirty Thirties, were an extremely hard time for the American people. Many people had bought items on credit, and now they had no money to pay it back. It was a time of bankruptcy and foreclosure. It was a time of breaking. All across America, families

Chapter 30

picked up their belongings and tried to find better places to live. As the economy sagged and cracked, the weather did nothing to help.

The 1930s wasone of the worst ecologically disastrous times in modern history. Decades of poor farming and grazing techniques finally took its toll on the land. The bread basket of the nation - the prairie lands and great plains that had become the country's great farmlands - was nothing but a huge bowl of dust. Dust storms carried millions of tons of topsoil on scorching, howling, cyclonic winds, scattering and burying entire towns. Rainfall declined, and temperatures increased, turning the once-fertile farmland into vast wastelands, littered with dead animals, deserted buildings, and ruined farm implements. Dust storm after dust storm roared through the plains. Between 1932 and 1939, about fifty dust storms, sometimes called "black blizzards," swept through the country every year.

During this horrible time, about 3.5 million Americans living on the great plains were driven away from their farms and homesteads. Some of these people, known as "Exodusters" traveled along Route 66 to California in search of work, many of them carrying everything they owned, piled in the back of their rickety jalopies. By 1933, the unemployment rate rose to 25%. As America's unemployment rate climbed, it seemed everyone was looking for a job. Companies went out of business by the hundreds, banks were closing, and 2 million homeless people wandered the United States. At its lowest point, the stock market had lost 89.2% of its all-time high. (2)

During the 1930s, people scraped together their pennies to spend on a little amusement and entertainment. Interestingly, the Great Depression was a boom time for the Hollywood movie making industry. Perhaps the movies were a brief reprieve from the harsh realities of life around them, because comedies were extremely popular during this time. The *Three Stooges*, *The Wizard of Oz*, and the fanciful and beautiful dancing movies were extremely well attended.

On December 7, 1941, the Japanese staged a surprise attack on the naval base in Pearl Harbor, Hawaii. The world had been engaged in World War 2 for quite some time before America entered it, and it was the sudden need for manufactured goods and a new focus on patriotism that pulled America abruptly out of the Great Depression.

Chapter 31 — America in World War 2

General Tojo

Adolf Hitler

Benito Mussolini

Joseph Stalin

On December 7, 1941, a day that will live in infamy, Japanese bombers staged a surprise attack on the naval base at Pearl Harbor, Hawaii, shattering America's isolation from the war. (We will not focus an exceeding amount of time on the causes of World War 2, as it requires a deeper probe into the world events of that time. We will instead focus on the American war involvement.*)

America, still numbed by the effects of the Great Depression, had been watching through drowsy eyelids as the world snarled and clashed. Adolf Hitler had risen to power in faraway Germany, and the details of the atrocities he and his Nazi party inflicted upon their own people struck fear in the hearts of humanity around the world. His hatred of Jews was staggering, and the torture he inflicted upon them was evil to the core. Hitler was not the only terrifying dictator intent on taking over the world, though.

In Italy, Benito Mussolini had risen on a political movement called fascism, a system which enables the government to rule through terror, and Japan was subjected to the harsh leadership of a dictator named General Hideki Tojo. In 1940, these three evil men led their nations to form the Axis Powers.

Another dictator, Joseph Stalin, controlled the Soviet Union from 1929 through 1953. Under Stalin's leadership, the Soviet Union moved from being a poverty-stricken nation to being an industrialized, military superpower. Yet Stalin's epic brutality cost millions of his own citizens' lives. Even though he aligned himself with the United States and Britain during World War 2, he was no true friend to the free world and caused major problems in

Chapter 31

the years following World War 2.

Before America was forced into the war, the Allies, which included Britain, France, and the Soviet Union, among others fought to keep the seemingly unstoppable German troops from advancing through the entirety of Europe. In the spring of 1940, the Germans conquered Norway, Denmark, the Netherlands, and Belgium, with Paris and much of France falling in June. Hitler seemed unstoppable. His intent desire was to have everything. As his men ransacked city after city, they were commanded to take the great artwork and sculptures of Europe. Museums containing all of the great artwork of history were emptied as Hitler's men stole and hid each country's treasures.

> "We look forward to a world founded upon four... human freedoms. The first is freedom of speech and expression- everywhere in the world. The second is freedom of every person to worship God in his own way... The third is freedom from want... The fourth is freedom from fear... anywhere in the world."
> Franklin D. Roosevelt, State of the Union speech,
> January 6, 1941

President Franklin D. Roosevelt took the office for the third time in 1941. (He was the first and only president to serve more than two terms in office.) Roosevelt knew that if the Nazis and Fascists were not stopped, the United States of America would be eventually be in big trouble. Many historians believe that Hitler was intent on conquering all of the big European powers in order to remove them from his way in his final and ultimate goal - the United States of America.

In 1941, Congress enacted the Lend-Lease Act, which allowed the United States to ship ammunition and other supplies to Britain and its allies without immediate payment. When the Japanese attacked Pearl Harbor, President Roosevelt immediately requested Congress to pass a declaration of war against Japan, which was followed by an Axis declaration of war against the United States.

After the United States had entered the war, automobile factories and other plants were transformed into defense plants to produce airplanes, ships, weapons, and many other needed supplies. By 1944, America's factories were producing many more armaments than

Chapter 31

those in all of the Axis nations combined. As in World War 1, Americans gladly put up with shortages in order to redirect materials to military usage. Gasoline was always in short supply, as were sugar, butter, coffee, and cheese. Families received ration books with stamps to buy their allotted food supply. Again, women left home to work in factories and in other jobs that the men usually filled.

Time line of American Involvement in WW2

1941
October:
- A German submarine sinks the U.S. warship, Reuben James, in the North Atlantic. Only 45 of the ship's crew members survive. This is the first American ship sunk in the war.

November:
- Japanese diplomats arrive in Washington to try to find ways to avoid war with the United States. At the same time, six Japanese aircraft carriers head toward Pearl Harbor to carry out a surprise attack.

December:
- Japan attacks Pearl Harbor.

1942
January:
- Manila, Philippines, falls to Japanese troops.

February:
- Japan bombs Darwin, Australia.

April:
- U.S. troops arrive in Australia. On the Bataan Peninsula, in the Philippines, U.S. and Filipino troops are captured and forced to surrender. Over 5,000 Americans die.
- In America, the government forces thousands of Japanese-Americans into relocation camps in isolated areas for fear of an uprising.

May:
- U.S. warships turn back a Japanese invasion heading for New Guinea, in the Battle of the Coral Sea.

Chapter 31

June:
- U.S. carrier-based aircraft stop a Japanese invasion of Midway, near Hawaii. U.S. dive-bombers sink four Japanese carriers. The Battle of Midway was the turning point of the Pacific War.

August:
- U.S. Marines fight the first battle in the Solomon Islands, in an "island hopping" campaign that would eventually bring them closer to Japan.

September:
- A Japanese aircraft, launched from a Japanese submarine drops fire bombs on a forest near Brookings, Oregon. This was the first bombing on the continental United States.

1943

January:
- U.S. and Australian troops end the Japanese attempt to take New Guinea.

April:
- U.S. code-breakers decodes a Japanese radio message are able to shoot down Admiral Yamamoto as he flies to the Solomon Islands.

May:
- All warships sunk at Pearl Harbor, except the U.S.S. Utah, U.S.S. Arizona, and U.S.S. Oklahoma, are repaired and returned to the sea.
- U.S. troops retake Attu and Adak, thus ending the Japanese presence in Alaska's Aleutian Islands.

June:
- A Japanese destroyer sinks a PT-109, commanded by John F. Kennedy. The survivors swim for five hours to a small island where they are rescued.

July:
- British and U.S. troops land in Sicily.

September:
- German troops seize Rome, even though Italy surrenders. Allied troops continue to fight.

1944

June:
- U.S. troops enter Rome. On June 6, 155,000 Allied troops land on the beaches of Normandy, France, to liberate Europe.

July:
- U.S. forces liberate Guam.

Chapter 31

August:
- American and French troops liberate Paris.

September:
- Future President George Bush is shot down near Okinawa. He is rescued by a U.S. submarine.

October:
- U.S. forces lands in the Philippines. Liberation begins.

November:
- U.S. troops begin a drive to reach the Rhine River, Germany.

December:
- German forces begin the Battle of the Bulge, the largest land battle by the U.S. army.

1945

January:
- The U.S. soldiers turn back the German troops, and go on to win the Battle of the Bulge.

February:
- U.S. Marines land on the island of Iwo Jima in the Bonin Islands. They fight to make it a base for the fighter planes.

March:
- B-29s bomb Tokyo, killing more than eighty thousand people.
- U.S. troops invade Okinawa. (Fighting here will continue until July when the U.S. won.)
- U.S. troops force their way across the Rhine River.
- U.S. troops liberate Manila, Philippines.
- U.S. Eighth Air Force bombers attack Berlin in the heaviest air raid made on the city.

April:
-U.S. soldiers free thirty-two thousand survivors from the Dachau concentration camp. (Adolf Hitler commits suicide.)

May 7th: Germany surrenders.

August:
- Atomic bombs are dropped on Hiroshima (Aug. 6), and Nagasaki (Aug. 9) Japan surrenders (Aug. 14)

September 2nd: Japanese officials sign the surrender document.

Chapter 31

* The world wars will be covered more in depth, from the world view point, in Volume 7 of this series. If you are a high schooler, who has not studied this time period in depth from a world view (and if you are not going to have time in your high school years to complete Volume 7 of this series), I suggest that you spend some time reading and researching, in order to educate yourself about these important events.

Chapter 32 — America in the Last 50 Years

The 1960s and 1970s are considered a time of progress and protest. Many types of progress were made in the fields of medicine and science, but many other types of progress were not at all positive. Up until now, the culture of our country had been formed by traditional values for the most part. Most families consisted of a father, mother and children. It was during the 1960s and 1970s that these traditions began to be openly questioned.

For example, although the women's rights movement had originated in the quest for the right to vote, throughout the years the movement had gradually changed its direction and purpose. In the 1960s, many women protested against these traditional moral values and what they perceived to be the restricting roles of wife and mother. Because many people were tired of the fighting in Vietnam and the Cold War with Russia, they became extreme pacifists. The American involvement in the Vietnam War became a point of much contention, and anti-war protest became common across America and in Western European countries, Australia and Japan. Protest became a culture fad for young people all over the country, as they formed protest groups, raging against the war and against what they considered to be old fashioned and restricting traditions. It was during this time that many young (and some older) people formed a type of "fringe" lifestyle, known as the Hippies.

The 1960s was a decade of experimentation. Drug addictions, children born to unwed parents and diseases all became more common. It was during this decade that the advances in the medical field aided the cause of "free love." The contraceptive pill, a form of birth-control, enabled unmarried people to do whatever they wanted without as much fear of unwanted pregnancies. Illegal drugs became a huge factor in the music and culture of the 1960s. The affects of this new fascination in the entertainment business had a terrible influence on American culture. If you listen to the music of this time period, you may notice that many of the song lyrics are laced with strange double meanings or are simply nonsense.

Chapter 32

The space race between America and the Soviets was still moving ahead. Their goal, to put a human on the moon, pushed space technology to grow in amazing leaps and bounds. The Soviet Union stunned the world by launching an unmanned space craft, and in 1961, they were the first to successfully travel into space. The race was on; President Kennedy responded to this news by declaring that Americans would be the first to put a man on the moon.

After President Kennedy was assassinated, the following presidents, President Lyndon Johnson and President Richard Nixon, continued the support of Kennedy's goal of putting an American on the moon by the end of the 1960s. On July 16, 1969, the *Apollo 11* spaceship, along with crew members, Neil Armstrong, Buss Aldrin, and Michael Collins, blasted off toward the moon, while millions of people all over the world watched on television. On July 20, the craft reached the moon, and the next day, Armstrong and Aldrin piloted the small landing craft, *Eagle*, to the surface of the moon. On July 21, 1969, Neil Armstrong stepped out of the Eagle and into history.

The 1960s brought about a huge change in the Civil Rights movement. There were still many white people who were prejudiced and feared the black people. Many whites broke laws that were in place to protect the blacks, by using corrupt law enforcement officers and judges to carry out their wishes. Black Americans were segregated against in a terrible ways. They were forced to use separate drinking fountains and were made to take the least desirable seat on buses. Black children could not go to school with white children and were forced to attend all-black schools, which were not funded well.

Some states, believing that they had the right to segregation, fought desegregation at a state level. One school district in Virginia decided to close all of their schools rather then integrate. Even though a law was passed in 1954 outlawing segregation in public schools, many school boards and staff members found ways around it. America, it seemed, would become a nation of two separate races. Would the integration that was longed for by so many patriotic Americans ever come? Would America become "a nation moving towards two societies - one black, one white, separate but unequal?" (You will be completing an in-depth research project about the American Civil Rights Movement.)

Chapter 32

The 1960s had begun with many Americans believing that they stood at the dawn of a golden age, but by the end of the decade, it seemed that the nation was falling apart. The Civil Rights movement was making strides in the right direction, but in so many other ways, the political atmosphere was disappointing. The "New Frontier," a package of laws that was meant to "eliminate injustice and inequality in the United States"(a) had run into the Southern Democrats' determination to block it whenever they could. Many Americans wondered what to expect as they entered the 1970s.

Some of the political happenings of the 1970s were exceptionally strange. Richard Nixon had been elected the thirty-seventh President of the United States, and because he was responsible for the ending American involvement in the Vietnam War, President Nixon was a popular president in his first term. However, when he was re-elected in 1972, his second term was rocked by scandal.

On June 17, 1972, five men broke into the Democratic National Committee Headquarters at the Watergate complex. After investigation, the Federal Bureau of Investigation connected the burglars to the 1972 Committee to Re-elect the President. Little by little, evidence was brought out against the President's staff, but instead of coming clean with his part in the scandal, President Nixon tried to cover it up.

On August 5, 1974, Americans were shocked when a tape recording made in the Oval Office by the president, a few days after the burglary, was released as evidence against the Nixon. The recording documented a conversation between the president and his aide conspiring to block investigation of the burglary. President Nixon was now facing impeachment, but instead decided to resign.

President Nixon's Vice President, Spiro Agnew, who was charged with criminal behavior in the various political offices which he had held, had been removed from office before the presidential resignation. Agnew resigned from the office of Vice President on October 10, 1973, and Gerald Ford became the Vice President in his place. When President Nixon resigned, Ford became the thirty-eighth President of the United States of America.

Chapter 32

The 1970s were also a time of economic hardship for many people. The United States was getting more than a third of its oil from foreign providers by the mid 1970s. These countries did not like that the United States was helping Israel in their war against Syria and Libya, and as a result, many of them cut off the oil supply for a few months. This caused huge shortages throughout the country. As the price of gas drove up the price of goods, the economy worsened, and Americans were having to adjust their lifestyles to meet these new limitations. It was not an uncommon sight to see cars lined up around the block waiting for their turn at the gas pump. Many gas stations often displayed signs that read "NO GAS."

This was the state of political affairs during the 1970s. There were many disturbing changes during this time. Our relationships with foreign countries were shaky in many ways, and by 1980, Americans were desperate for a change. The economy had gone from bad, at the beginning of the 70s, to horrible by the end of that decade. Inflation was worse than it had been since the Great Depression. To make matters worse, there was a constant threat of nuclear war. The 1970s had ended with a hostage situation in Iran, with Muslim extremists holding over fifty Americans hostage with the intent to overthrow the reigning Shah of Iran. It was a long and complicated process, which ended in the hostages being released after four hundred forty-four days of captivity.

In the Presidential elections of 1980, Ronald Reagan, our fortieth President, was elected. President Reagan approached the economic crisis head on. It was his opinion that government should be much smaller than what it had become under the presidents of the 1970s. By the mid 80s, the country had responded to the change in the White House, and President Reagan was fast becoming a hero in the conservative camp. His governing method, sometimes called "Reaganomics," promoted individual achievement. In 1982, oil prices dropped, which greatly helped the economy in its upswing. President Reagan also worked to build up America's defenses. He warned that America needed to be a formidable power to be reckoned with, and he built up the armed forces and America's arsenal of nuclear weapons.

The 1980s were a time of many important political happenings. President Reagan was instrumental in bringing about the end of the Cold War. The president and the Soviet Union

Chapter 32

leader, Mikhail Gorbachev, held peace talks, easing the tensions between the two super-power countries. In 1987, President Reagan stood in front of the Berlin Wall* and declared, "There is one sign the Soviets can make that would be unmistakable, that would advance dramatically the cause of freedom and peace." He then called upon his Soviet counterpart: "Secretary General Gorbachev, if you seek peace--if you seek prosperity for the Soviet Union and Eastern Europe--if you seek liberalization: come here, to this gate. Mr. Gorbachev, open this gate. Mr. Gorbachev, tear down this wall." President Reagan left office after serving two terms. Reagan's Vice President, George H. Bush, won the 1988 elections and took office on January 20, 1989.

*In 1945, after Germany's defeat in World War II, Berlin, the country's capital was divided into four sections. The Americans, British and French controlled the Western region, and the Soviets controlled the Eastern region. The three Western sections came together to form the Federal Republic of Germany, or West Germany, in May, 1949. The German Democratic Republic, or East Germany was established in October, 1949. In 1952, the border between the two countries was closed, and East Germans had to ask permission to leave their country. In August 1961, the East German government built the Berlin Wall to prevent its citizens from escaping to freedom in the West. This wall had stood as a dividing line between Communist countries and free countries in Europe. The Berlin Wall toppled in 1989.

Appendix

Please leave blank.

Conscientious Conclusion Projects

Conscientious Conclusion Projects consist of four parts - something I like to call: **R⁴**

    Research -> GO DEEP!
    Read   -> GO to the sources!
    Reason -> Get to the root!
    Relate   -> Give your thoughts - be articulate! (Either write about what you find or do an oral presentation for at least your family.)

You will be completing four **Conscientious Conclusion Projects** this year. As you complete them, check them off here.

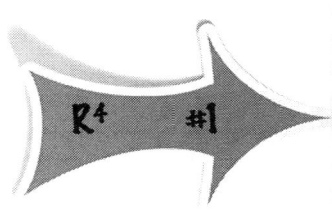

Date completed: _____

-> What was the role of the Bible in the founding of our country? <-

Starting at the Pilgrims and coming up through the early years of our new country's "experimental" government, research, read, reason, and relate.

Hints...
- Research the Geneva Bible
- What was the original reason for the Public School? (You might find reading "Common Sense" by Thomas Paine quite helpful.)

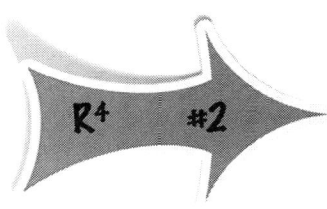

Date completed: _____

-> What is the Matrix of Liberty? <-

Who built/designed it? Where is it? What is its purpose? Why do you suppose most Americans do not know what it is?

Hints...
- The movie, "Monumental," goes into detail about this monument. (This movie was produced by Kirk Cameron and is available in many places.)

Conscientious Conclusion Projects

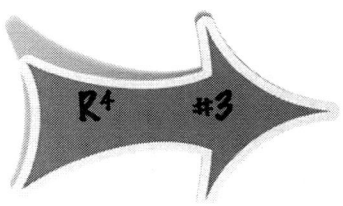

Date completed:
_____

->Separation of Church and State<-

Where did this phrase originate? Who said/wrote it? To whom? In what context? How is it used today?

Hints...
- Research a certain letter Thomas Jefferson wrote.

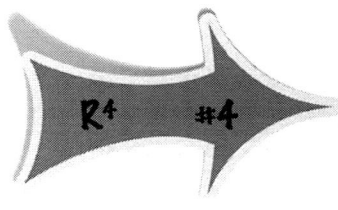

Date completed:
_____

->Original Purpose for the U.S. Government<-

How big was our government originally supposed to be? In what ways has it become "too big for its britches"?

Hints...
- Research the original limitations put on our government.

Works cited

Chapter 1
(1) page 46, Living Biographies of Famous Men, by Henry Thomas and Dana LeeThomas, Garden City Publishing Co., Inc. Garden City, New York, copyright 1944

Chapter 10
Dr. Rush (1) (DTH Foundations of Character DVD) by David Barton, Focus on the Family, 2006

Chapter 11

1. John Adams: www.wallbuilders.com, visited 11/15/13
(a) Thomas Jefferson, The Writings of Thomas Jefferson (Washington D.C. The Thomas Jefferson Memorial Association, 1904), Vol. XIII, p. 292-294. In a letter from John Adams to Thomas Jefferson on June 28, 1813.
(b) John Adams, The Works of John Adams, Second President of the United States, Charles Francis Adams, editor (Boston: Little Brown and Company, 1856), Vol. X, p. 254, to Thomas Jefferson on April 19, 1817
(c) John Adams, 14 November, 1760. Diary

2. Samuel Adams:
(d) www.samuel-adams-heritage.com visited 2/22/14

3. Josiah Bartlett:
(e) Proclamation for a Day of Fasting and Prayer, March 17, 1792, Josiah Bartlett

4. Alexander Hamilton:
(f) www.goodreads.com
(g) http://www.westillholdthesetruths.org

5. Thomas Jefferson
(h) http://www.constitution.org

6. James Madison:
(k) quote found at www.wallbuilders.com on 2/24/2014. Quote from: The Debates and Proceedings in the Congress of the United States 451, 1st Cong;, 1st Sess. (Washington, D.C. : Gales & Seaton 1834) (June 15, 1789)
(l) Written to William Bradford on November 9,1772. James Madison

Works cited

7. George Washington
(m)(n) www.goodreads.com/author/quotes/4356.George_Washington , George Washington, visited on 2/2/14

Chapter 13
(1) (Government 101, page 6, copyright 2010, Laura Petrisin)

Chapter 28
(1) http://www.wallbuilders.com/libissuesarticles.asp?id=95, paragraph 7 and 9, David Barton - 01/2001, visited on 3/6/14

Chapter 30
(1) http://www.stockpickssystem.com/the-great-depression/ paragraph 4, (posted on April 25, 2011, by Tom DeGrace) website visited 3/10/14
(2) http://www.stockpickssystem.com/the-great-depression/ paragraph 7, (posted on April 25, 2011, by Tom DeGrace) website visited 3/10/14

Chapter 32
(a) http://www.history.com/topics/1960s, paragraph 2, visited on 3/12/14

Teacher's Notes

Supplemental resources we have to go with this course:

Teacher's Notes

Made in the USA
Lexington, KY
26 July 2016